LUNAR

NODES

About the Author

Wendell C. Perry is an astrologer and artist with fifty years of experience studying the mysteries of this vast and wonderful universe. He is the author of several books on astrology and a frequent contributor to *The Mountain Astrologer*. You can follow his ever-evolving ideas and whimsies on his blog at goodgollyastrology.com.

What They Mean
and How They
Affect Your Life

LUNAR

NODES

Wendell C. Perry

author of *Behind the Horoscope*

Llewellyn Publications | Woodbury, Minnesota

FIRST EDITION
First Printing, 2022

Book design by Christine Ha
Cover design by Shannon McKuhen

Llewellyn Publications is a registered trademark of Llewellyn Worldwide Ltd.

Library of Congress Cataloging-in-Publication Data
Names: Perry, Wendell, author.
Title: Lunar nodes : what they mean and how they affect your life / Wendell
    Perry, author of Behind the horoscope.
Description: First edition. | Woodbury, Minnesota : Llewellyn Publications,
    2022. | Includes bibliographical references.
Identifiers: LCCN 2021051315 (print) | LCCN 2021051316 (ebook) | ISBN
    9780738770086 | ISBN 9780738770161 (ebook)
Subjects: LCSH: Moon—Miscellanea. | Human beings—Effect of the moon on.
Classification: LCC BF1723 .P47 2022 (print) | LCC BF1723 (ebook) | DDC
    133.5/32—dc23/eng/20211106
LC record available at https://lccn.loc.gov/2021051315
LC ebook record available at https://lccn.loc.gov/2021051316

Llewellyn Worldwide Ltd. does not participate in, endorse, or have any authority or responsibility concerning private business transactions between our authors and the public.

All mail addressed to the author is forwarded but the publisher cannot, unless specifically instructed by the author, give out an address or phone number.

Any internet references contained in this work are current at publication time, but the publisher cannot guarantee that a specific location will continue to be maintained. Please refer to the publisher's website for links to authors' websites and other sources.

Llewellyn Publications
A Division of Llewellyn Worldwide Ltd.
2143 Wooddale Drive
Woodbury, MN 55125-2989
www.llewellyn.com

Printed in the United States of America

Other Books by Wendell C. Perry

*Behind the Horoscope: How the Placement of
the Sun & Moon Tells a Story About You*

Father Sun, Mother Moon: Astrology's Dynamic Duo

Saturn Cycles: Mapping the Changes in Your Life

*The Mars/Venus Affair: Astrology's Sexiest Planets
(with Linda Perry)*

This book is dedicated to my wife, Linda,
who taught me how to write a meaningful
sentence and so much more.

Contents

PART
ONE

This is a book about the mystery of the Nodes of the Moon. Part of that mystery involves reincarnation and past lives, but it also extends to things like fate and karma and the relationship between our individual consciousness and the overarching consciousness that pervades the universe. The Lunar Nodes represent a gateway into that mystery. It is a gateway that is provided to each one of us, and this book is designed to help guide you through it.

In discussing this gateway and the mystery beyond, I have tried to keep things as concrete and simple as possible. I talk about behaviors and attributes that have relevance to the real world of human affairs. But there's always a limit to what words can do, so I also employ archetypical images like the Hero and the Trickster to help us in our understanding. The goal is not to define the mystery. It is only to give the reader a hint as to its breadth and grandeur.

In order to explore this mystery, I make extensive use of aspects to the Lunar Nodes by the Sun, the Moon, and the planets in your horoscope. In chapter 1, I explain what aspects are and how they work with the Nodes of the Moon. However, in order to know which aspects are relevant to your natal horoscope, I recommend having your astrological chart prepared. Such a horoscope chart can be obtained free of charge from several providers on the internet. One of the most commonly used is Astrolabe (alabe.com). You can also contact me at goodgollyastrology.com, and I will provide you with a chart.

Once you have the chart, you can identify the Nodes of the Moon by their glyph: ☊ for the North Node and ☋ for the South Node. A simple way of spotting aspects to the Nodes (if they are not already marked) is to scan the chart for any planet (along with the Sun and Moon) that is at or near the same degree as the Nodes of the Moon. For example, if the Lunar Nodes are at 26 degrees of a sign, then any planet at 26 degrees (or thereabouts) of any sign will be in aspect to the Nodes.

It is always good to have the time of birth when getting a horoscope done, but for aspects to the Lunar Nodes, this is typically only necessary for aspects by the Moon (which moves around 12 degrees in twenty-four hours). So, if you don't know your time of birth and don't have any way of finding it out (such as your birth certificate, a birth announcement, or the memory of a family member), you can have the chart done for noon on your birth date (or for an approximate time, if you have it). This will give you a pretty good idea of what planets are aspecting the Nodes. It will also provide you with the sign placement of the Nodes of the Moon. However, knowing the house placement requires a precise time of birth.

Once you are armed with a horoscope, complete or not, you are ready to tackle the mystery of the Lunar Nodes. There is a lot to learn. At the same time, there is a lot of fun to be had. After all, you're exploring the nooks and crannies of the greatest mystery. What could be more exciting than that?

CHAPTER 1

A New Way of Looking at Lunar Nodes

Let's start by defining our terms. What are the Lunar Nodes or Nodes of the Moon? First of all, they are not planets or heavenly bodies. You will not see them hovering above you in the sky on a warm summer night. You will not see them at any time. The Nodes of the Moon are abstract points in space where the orbit of the Moon around the Earth intersects the apparent orbit of the Sun. This intersection takes place at two points in the sky directly opposite one another. One of these points is labeled the North Node of the Moon, the other the South Node.

Even though they may just be creations of celestial mathematics, a few times each year the Lunar Nodes demonstrate their importance in dramatic fashion. When the Sun and the Moon pass through one or both of these abstract points at the same time, we get a solar or Lunar eclipse, events that sent primitive humans running for their caves and that still fascinate sky watchers today. Witnessing an eclipse, we get an idea of why the astrologers of ancient India described the nodal axis as a ravenous dragon with its head (known as Rahu) represented by the North Node and its tail (called Ketu) represented by the South Node.

During an eclipse, we get an inkling of the power of the Nodes of the Moon, but also of their mystery. In general, this book is about that mystery. In particular, this book looks at the aspects made to the Nodes of the Moon by the Sun, Moon, and planets in a horoscope.

The term *aspect* refers to the distance between two celestial bodies as measured in degrees along the ecliptic. Astrologers consider some of those measurements to be significant, in particular 0 degrees (conjunction), 30 degrees (semi-sextile), 60 degrees (sextile), 90 degrees (square), 120 degrees (trine), 150 degrees (quincunx), and 180 degrees (opposition). In part 1 of this book, we examine the meaning of these aspects to the Nodes of the Moon in the natal horoscope.

What Do the Lunar Nodes Mean?

For most astrologers, the meaning of the Nodes of the Moon relates strongly to the concept of reincarnation. Astrologers in India have been using the Nodes as descriptors of previous incarnations of the soul for centuries, and, in more recent times, the practice has become commonplace in Western astrology. The Nodes of the Moon are seen as indicators of past life experiences and karmic influences.

I (like so many people) find the idea of reincarnation and past lives fascinating. However, I also see limitations to this approach. For one thing, it focuses on the past. There are astrologers who feel that it is only by understanding traumas experienced in past lives that we can get to the root of psychological and spiritual blockages in the present. Yet, when you think about the short, brutal lives that most of our ancestors lived—with war, famine, and pestilence a constant presence—it seems likely that we would all come into this life with more past life traumas than we could ever count. Yes, some of us may benefit from dealing with one particular past life trauma that has relevance to our horoscope and our circumstances in this life, but the rest of us might be better served looking to the present and the future.

This does not mean that this book dismisses the relationship between the Lunar Nodes and reincarnation or that I won't be discussing reincarnation. However, I think we also have to leave the door open to other ideas and other mysteries. We have to consider the possibility that there are multiple forces shaping our fate and our soul's journey through this life, forces that might be beyond our immediate comprehension. Any discussion of the Nodes of the Moon has to include the idea that they represent a gateway, not just to past lives, but to the even greater enigma of the relationship between our human consciousness and the universe.

All of that sounds very mystical and, when we talk about the Nodes of the Moon, we do get into territory that can be numinous and hard to define. For this reason, I focused my study on the behaviors and trends of various people who could be observed and described in real-life terms. I wanted to know how aspects to the Nodes of the Moon influenced the personality and character of an individual, and I wanted to base my observations, as much as possible, on demonstrable facts.

Examples

In the course of doing the research on which this book is based, I studied the aspects to the Lunar Nodes in well over one thousand timed horoscopes, plus a hundred or so charts in which the time of birth was unknown or in doubt. These were all the horoscopes of so-called celebrities, people about whom I could acquire information through published sources. There is a built-in bias that comes with using celebrity examples. They all have at least one common characteristic: they are famous. That typically means that they were, or are, especially ambitious, enterprising, and/or gifted with special talents. However, in order to do this kind of research, you need people whose lives have been examined and described, preferably by an unbiased third party. You hope for serious and observant biographers, but interviews and articles in the popular press or online can also be helpful.

I looked at so many examples because I wanted to test certain assumptions we have about the way the Nodes of the Moon work. For example, when Western astrologers look at the Nodes of the Moon in the context of reincarnation, they typically make a strong distinction between the North Node and the South Node. The South Node is supposed to represent behaviors held over from a past life that might restrict our future spiritual development.

These are skills, attributes, and habits that might come easily to us but, on a spiritual level, hold us back. The North Node, on the other hand, shows us the things we need to work on to advance our spiritual development. It is where we develop new skills and find new experiences that will make us a stronger, wiser, and more spiritually aware person.

I have to admit that I've always been fond of this application of the Lunar Nodes, and I have used it with some success in the past. When I began this research, I tried hard to make a qualitative distinction between aspects that were more focused on the North Node and aspects that focused on the South Node. However, in terms of the behaviors and attitudes displayed by my examples, this distinction didn't seem to apply. I finally had to admit that, at least when it came to aspects, there was no obvious difference between the Nodes. Venus on the South Node seemed to function in much the same way as Venus on the North Node. The only exception was with the Sun aspecting the Nodes, and I will discuss that in depth in chapters 2 and 3.

This is not to say that, on a spiritual level, there is no difference in meaning between an aspect to the North and South Node. We can't assume that everything that is important to an individual happens in the public sphere. However, those internal, spiritual levels are not generally open to this kind of research. We have to go with what we can see, with the behaviors displayed and the attitudes expressed. It is always possible that these are not truly representative of that person's spiritual life, but who can say they know that for sure?

I should add that when I began examining the influence of the Nodes in the signs and astrological houses, I found that the distinction between the North and South Nodes did apply. I'll have more to say about that in part 2.

Consistency

Another thing that I learned from looking at all these examples is that there was a marked lack of consistency in the way in which aspects to the Nodes of the Moon worked. There were many examples in which the influence of the aspects to the Lunar Nodes was emphatic, and many others in which it was difficult to discern. This is a common issue in any astrological research.

The horoscope is a complex document, and indicators often contradict one another. A placement of the Sun that seems to describe extraordinary self-confidence might be countered in the same horoscope by an aspect to the Sun that brings tendencies toward anxiety and self-doubt. The process of working through these contradictions is what life is all about. However, for the researcher, these contradictions can obscure what might otherwise be a clearly defined tendency. They guarantee that there are going to be plenty of hits and plenty of misses in any list of people with a particular aspect or placement.

However, even though I was aware of these problems, I felt that what was happening with the aspects to the Nodes of the Moon was something different. The horoscope gives us a map of a person's consciousness. How this consciousness is displayed to the world can vary depending on many factors, such as genetics, cultural influences, and social position, but, beneath all that, it is the person's consciousness that forms the basis for their personality, individuality, and self. The inconsistency with which these aspects to the Nodes worked caused me to question what the Nodes of the Moon have to add to this map of consciousness and exactly how that contribution functions relative to the rest of that individual's personality.

Guests

The answer to that question is that what comes to us through the Nodes of the Moon is separate from the basic construct we call personality. In this sense, the Nodes represent an outlier, a hidden influence that comes into our lives and our individual consciousness from a broader consciousness that pervades the universe. While the rest of the horoscope describes us in psychological terms— based on our earthly experiences and how we react to and internalize those experiences—the Nodes of the Moon serve as a gateway that links that basic personality with matters more cosmic and transcendent, like memories of past lives, our spiritual evolution, and the mystery of karma and fate.

This is why the influence of aspects to the Nodes seems so inconsistent. Since they are not part of the basic structure of the personality, they function within our lives like guests or visitors from the cosmic beyond. They stand apart from the basic construct of the personality. They don't shape or change that personality. Instead, they work with the structure that already exists. In some cases, these guests might find tendencies within that personality that blend nicely with their purpose. In others, they might be hobbled by contrary tendencies. Like a guest, the influence of the Nodes might also seem to come and go. If the circumstances during one period of your life are not conducive to the Node's purposes, it might return and make that influence felt during another period.

When one of these guests or hidden influencers is active in your life, especially if its influence is supported by other factors in your horoscope, it might seem to exert a power that supplants what you regard as your essential character. You may find yourself in situations in which you are overwhelmed by outside forces and your hopes and aspirations seem to have little relevance. This can make these visitors seem more like rude intruders than welcome guests. At the same time, these hidden influencers often provide us with special talents and attributes that seem to come from a separate place, a place that has little to do with our background or our character. These aspects are our gateway to a greater awareness and a power beyond our paltry sense of reality. They are our link to those grand concepts we call archetypes.

Archetypes

What the planets aspecting the Lunar Nodes in our horoscope show us are the archetypes that are coming into our lives through that gateway. An archetype is an image or idea that holds a place in the consciousness of all human beings, regardless of their cultural heritage. In astrology, we see the meaning of each of the signs and planets as a representative of one of these archetypical figures. It is the interaction of these archetypes that makes up the bulk of every horoscope interpretation. Planets aspecting the Nodes of the Moon in your horoscope describe archetypes with which you have a special relationship. You relate to them in a way that is different from how they function as planets or signs in your horoscope. Through aspects to your Lunar Nodes, you are introduced to these archetypes in a form that is closer to their ultimate mystery, perhaps because they come to you as past life experiences or as fate, karma, or an important step in your spiritual development.

Defining these archetypes in a clear and concise way is impossible. They have existed through the ages and have shown up in countless myths and stories in different guises and with many different names. What follows is a brief description of the archetypes we will meet in this book. This is not intended to define these archetypes—only to illuminate the way they interact with the Nodes of the Moon.

- *The Sun:* The pure expression of vitality, enterprise, and ego. It is the Star, the Hero, and the Leader.
- *The Moon:* The Moon is often seen as the Mother. But a mother is not a mother without a child, and it is as the Child that we meet this archetype when it aspects the Lunar Nodes.
- *Mercury:* As it is in Roman mythology, Mercury is the Messenger, the carrier of information and knowledge.
- *Venus:* Though generally termed the goddess of beauty, in aspect to the Nodes, Venus signifies the power of the Divine Feminine.
- *Mars:* Mars is simple: Mars is the drive, competitive spirit, and pure rage of the Warrior.
- *Jupiter:* As an archetype, Jupiter brings us the great comfort of faith—in a god, a leader, a political program, or our own inevitable good fortune.
- *Saturn:* Saturn answers Jupiter's faith with doubt. It is the stern Teacher who shows us all our deficiencies and then asks, "What are you going to do about it?"
- *Uranus:* Uranus is the Trickster, the Contrarian, and the Disrupter. The Norse knew this archetype well. They called it Loki.
- *Neptune:* Neptune is the archetype who allows us to transcend the ordinary and visualize a new and better reality.
- *Pluto:* Pluto guards the gateway to our transformation. We meet this archetype with dread and come away from it, often, with a greater wisdom.

Understanding these archetypes and how they function when aspecting the Nodes of the Moon offers you a greater understanding of yourself. They can also bring you a greater understanding of how your consciousness fits into a broader universal consciousness. This is true whether you relate the Node of the Moon to past life experiences or something else. These simple features of celestial mechanics, bringing together the emotional Moon with the dynamic Sun, represent the eternal link between our mundane lives and our divine aspirations. Finding out how aspects to the Nodes work in your horoscope is the key to understanding the relationship between you as an individual and that great mystery that underlies all existence. That is something, I think, that is definitely worth discussing.

Ground Rules

Though I described what astrologers mean by "aspect" earlier in this chapter, it might be good to define it in greater depth. The term *aspect* refers to the relationship between two or more planets in a horoscope as measured by degrees of the zodiac. Aspects to nonplanetary factors in the horoscope, such as the Nodes of the Moon, are also considered important. Aspects show us how planets or points in the horoscope relate to another. A square aspect (90 degrees), for example, generally describes a stressful relationship that often features conflict. A trine (120 degrees), on the other hand, describes an easy and typically positive relationship.

That's the way aspects function in a horoscope. Each one has its own special dynamic. However, aspects to the Lunar Nodes seem to function in a way that is quite different. The nature of the aspect—conjunction (0 degrees), semi-sextile (30 degrees), sextile (60 degrees), square (90 degrees), trine (120 degrees), quincunx (150 degrees), and opposition (180 degrees)—doesn't seem to matter. "Hard" aspects, like squares or oppositions, function much the same as "easy" aspects, like trines and sextiles. What matters is that the archetype represented by that planet has been given a special importance in your life.

Now that you have some basic knowledge of the ground rules, you are ready to begin your journey. It is a journey in which you will meet a lot of interesting people. We'll call them archetypes, of course, but they have the same quirks and range of behaviors that we expect from human beings. And why shouldn't they? They are approximations made by human minds of forces far beyond human comprehension. You've probably met many of them already in the course of your life. You might have had a boss who was a Hero or a Warrior or a friend who had both the charm and the infuriating lack of self-control of the Child. However, the ones that you really need to meet are the ones nestled inside your horoscope and aspecting your Lunar Nodes. These are the guests, the hidden influencers that you most need to understand, because they are the ones who connect your existence on this tiny planet called Earth with the great mystery of everything else.

CHAPTER 2

The Sun Aspecting
the North Node

*Technical Node—Because the Lunar Nodes are always 180 degrees apart,
any aspect to one is an aspect to both. In distinguishing aspects to the North
Node from aspects to the South Node, I chose the aspects that I regarded as
strongest. For the North Node, that was the conjunction (0 degrees), the square
(90 degrees), the trine (120 degrees), and the quincunx (150 degrees).
The subject of orbs will be explained in chapter 14.*

The Sun comes to us wearing the trappings of royalty. Such is its brightness, such is its splendor, that we dare not look at it directly. Sometimes we bask in its warmth. Other times, we are blistered by its intensity. In either case, the Sun doesn't seem to care. It glares down on us from above, mighty and distant. And yet, it is our beacon, the light we follow across the sky. It brings us life and illumination, and when it disappears beneath the horizon at nightfall, we mourn.

In the horoscope, the Sun is the embodiment of ego—the dynamic, outward-reaching self—and it therefore holds sway over a big chunk of our identity. Its sign, aspects, and house placement are all major determiners of who we are. The meaning of the Sun as an archetype, however, stands separate from what it says about your character and your sense of self. It is still very much about ego, but it is ego in its essence—as the focal point of pride, inspiration, and power—that has little to do with the identity of any single person.

The archetypical figures that embody this solar energy demand our attention. They are the Star, the Hero, and the Leader.

The Star

Some people with the Sun aspecting the North Node welcome this guest with open arms. This is usually because the rest of their horoscope contains strong indicators of self-esteem and flamboyance. The dynamic energy of this archetype takes those basic attributes up a notch and imposes upon them its own pride and thirst for attention. It makes the person with that horoscope a star.

We see evidence of this star mentality and exaggerated ego in the careers and personalities of several people born with the Sun conjunct the North Node, such as President Donald Trump, radio host Howard Stern, British Prime Minister Boris Johnson, and financier J. Pierpont Morgan. The personality of the last man was once compared to an oncoming locomotive. But was it really Morgan's personality this biographer was seeing or just the Sun as an archetype sufficiently empowered?

Other aspects to the North Node by the Sun also bring us similar people known for their ego. Benito Mussolini and Oliver Cromwell had the square. So does Marshall Mathers, better known as Eminem. Napoleon Bonaparte, Theodore Roosevelt, Roy Cohn, and John D. Rockefeller Sr. had the trine. Most of these examples had other factors in their horoscope that could indicate egotism, such as personal planets in Leo or strongly aspected by Jupiter. In these horoscopes, the archetype found a comfortable home and made the most of it.

Of course, the people named here are connected by something other than aspects to the Nodes. All of them are men. Our culture makes it much easier for men to express the power of the solar archetype than it does for women. However, if you look hard enough, you can also find women who have expressed the self-confidence and affection for the spotlight provided by this archetype.

With the conjunction, we have the flamboyant businesswoman Leona Helmsley, noted for her dismissive attitude toward "the little people" and taxes. With the square, we have the daring photographer Margaret Bourke-White, noted for both the artistry of her work and her willingness to face danger and hardship to get the right shot. With the trine, we have the outspoken congresswoman Alexandria Ocasio-Cortez and possibly (depending on what year of birth you use) the indomitable Mae West.

As these examples demonstrate, the Star mentality can lead a person to wealth, fame, or political prominence, but it can also result in ruin and infamy. One example of this with the conjunction is Michael Avenatti. Avenatti rose to prominence in 2017 as the lawyer for Stormy Daniels in her case against Donald Trump. For a while, Avenatti was a star and a fixture on television news. He even floated the idea of running for president. Then a variety of legal problems cropped up in Avenatti's life, and his notoriety took a darker turn.

An even more famous example of someone who let his affinity for this archetype take him to a bad end is Charlie Sheen, who has the square. When Sheen launched his "winning" tour in 2011 after being fired from his extremely popular sitcom, he was expressing all the hubris and lack of self-awareness of the Star archetype at its worst.

The Hero

For the Stars, being the center of attention is just a natural outgrowth of their charm, charisma, and powerful personality. There is another variation of this archetype, however, that seeks to earn that adulation through extraordinary acts of courage and heroism. This is the kind of courage and heroism that allowed baseball great Hank Aaron (with the conjunction) to shrug off racist slurs and death threats and break Babe Ruth's record for home runs, the kind of courage that took John Glenn (with the square) into space and caused a cavalry officer named Manfred von Richthofen (with the conjunction) to trade his horse for an airplane and become the Red Baron, Germany's most feared ace during World War I.

Courage can come from many sources within the personality and within the horoscope. The courage we see from people with the Sun aspecting the

North Node comes out of a conviction that they have been put on this earth to do something significant and that no enemy, opposition, or obstacle is sufficient to stop them from fulfilling that destiny. This awareness might be rooted in a past life experience, but for the Hero, it is simply there, a voice that tells them they will not be defeated. Of course, that voice can occasionally be wrong. The famous Red Baron was eventually shot down.

There are different types of courage and different ways of becoming a hero. Some people with the Sun conjunct the North Node become heroes because they represent a higher power or a greater wisdom. They are mystics and people of faith, like Pope Francis I, Baba Ram Dass, and Thomas Moore (author of *Care of the Soul*). These three men turned the power of ego into a spiritual force. They found in ego something that the presidents and billionaires miss. They discovered the power that can come out of merging our individual egos with the cosmic, with a force that is inside us and permeates everything outside us. Is there a kind of egotism in saying that you have a special relationship with God, the Buddha, or the spiritual in general? Perhaps. But, at its best, it is an egotism that has been purified by study, self-examination, and self-discipline. It is an egotism that creates the best sort of heroes: heroes who can teach and inspire us.

We see some of this sort of heroism in the writings of Helena Blavatsky and in the work of her successor as head of the Theosophical Society, Annie Besant (both with the conjunction). We also see it in the lives of inspirational figures whose aims were much more secular, such as Eleanor Roosevelt. We see it in the courage and determination of both Martin Luther, who had the trine, and Martin Luther King Jr., who had the quincunx.

Of course, just because you see yourself as a hero, that doesn't automatically make you one. There may be some disagreement or doubt about the heroic nature of your actions. Edward Snowden, who has the Sun conjunct the North Node, was identifying himself strongly with this solar archetype when he released evidence of excessive government surveillance of the online chatter of innocent American citizens. Unfortunately for him, the citizenry was not impressed. They were, in general, willing to sacrifice their privacy for the sake of security. Instead of being celebrated as a hero, Snowden became a wanted criminal and was forced to live in exile.

The Leader

Another manifestation of the solar archetype is the Leader. People who are heroes and people who are stars often turn out to be leaders, as well. We see this in many of the examples previously listed, like Martin Luther King Jr., Napoleon, or Oliver Cromwell. It is only natural that we look to people with extraordinary self-confidence and people who inspire us with their courage for leadership. People with the Sun aspecting the North Node often feel that they were born to lead and, as the examples presented here indicate, they frequently rise to positions of leadership.

With the Sun conjunct the North Node, we have three men who were actually born to rule: Francis I and Louis XV of France and Charles II of England. We also have two US presidents: Ronald Reagan with the conjunction, and Theodore Roosevelt with the trine. Outside the United States, we have the British Prime Minister Boris Johnson; Salvador Allende, who was the president of Chile before he was overthrown and killed in a military coup; and Jair Bolsonaro, the bombastic president of Brazil.

It isn't just in the political arena that people with the Sun aspecting the North Node of the Moon lead. They can also lead by being on the cutting edge of the arts and in the world of ideas. André Breton was the self-anointed leader to the Surrealist poets and painters in Paris during the 1920s and '30s, and he defended his position by any means necessary, including clubbing rivals with his cane. Antoni Gaudi became a leader by creating a style of architecture that had never been seen before. Bob Fosse did similar things with dance, and Jackie Chan with martial arts.

Of course, there are a lot of great leaders who did not have the Sun aspecting the North Node. The attributes for leadership can come from many sources in the horoscope, factors rooted in the individual's character and personality. What the archetype brings is something different. Often what puts people with these aspects to the North Node in positions of power has less to do with their abilities or character than with fortuitous circumstances. Louis XV survived both a smallpox and a measles epidemic that took out all the claimants to the throne in front of him. Charles II rode the waves of revolution and counter-revolution to secure his place on the throne. Fate often seems to play a role in the advancement of people with these aspects. Theodore Roosevelt was thrust into the presidency after the assassination of President William McKinley. Robert Kennedy had devoted his life to advancing the career of his charismatic brother. It was only after John Kennedy's assassination that he stepped into the spotlight.

What is the secret behind the fateful events that puts so many people with the Sun aspecting the North Node in the right place at the right time? We might presume that it is a product of karma or that the person was reliving a pattern set in a past life. What we can know, however, is that people with these aspects often have a special relationship with destiny.

The Archetype and You

With regard to past lives, aspects by the Sun to the Nodes of the Moon are typically considered indications of a royal linage. The idea is that, in a past life, you held a position of leadership, or at least privilege, that has been carried forward in this life as an exalted sense of self-worth. You seek to be a star, a hero, or a leader in your current incarnation because, having had a taste of glory and adulation, you long to return to the spotlight. Of course, history is filled with stars, heroes, and leaders who rose to great heights only to suffer an ignoble and, sometimes, extremely painful decline. Would these poor souls really want to repeat that process? Maybe, instead, they would prefer a quieter and less glorious life.

Regardless of what might have happened to you in a past life, if you were born with the Sun aspecting the North Node of the Moon, you have come into this life looking for a place to shine. More importantly, you have come into this life with the assumption that it is your right to shine. There may be factors within your horoscope that argue against that assumption, that tell you to sit down and be quiet. As a result, this archetype could get pushed to the side and ignored. This arrangement might seem workable for you, but it will never be completely comfortable. This influencer, hidden though it may be, doesn't go away. It is likely that it will find some way at some time in your life to slip past your doubts and take a bow.

Another factor to keep in mind is that the influence of this archetype can be compartmentalized, so that it shows strongly at certain times or in certain activities or with certain people, but otherwise it is not evident at all. Maybe you're a leader at work, a hero when you're with your kids, or a star after a couple of beers at your local bar. It might be issues from a past life that cause certain situations or certain people to bring the solar archetype to the foreground. In any case, people who know you in other circumstances— circumstances in which the archetype is quiet—might see this side of you and wonder what happened. You might even wonder about it yourself.

Even those of you who don't feel like a star or a leader or a hero can still be called to take on one of these roles by some sudden turn of events in your life. You might resist and complain. You might be plagued by self-doubt. But in situations in which leadership or heroism is required, you will feel compelled to provide it. This could just mean standing up for a principle or belief that might be unpopular or controversial. When Ellen DeGeneres (who has the square) came out as gay, she wasn't trying to be a hero or a leader. She was just speaking the truth. Sometimes that's all it takes to exercise the heroism or star power with these aspects.

All the examples cited here have been famous, but fame is not a necessary byproduct of these aspects. People with the Sun aspecting the Lunar Nodes don't need to see their name in lights. They just need to exercise the attributes of this archetype in whatever context they can. You can be a star, a hero, or a leader within the confines of your own community, your work, your union, or your church. The applause of your friends, family, and work mates may be all that is required to make this archetypical guest happy.

Of course, we must also acknowledge that things can go wrong, that there are instances in which this archetype pushes people beyond their natural capacity or draws from them the worst of their character. Of the many famous leaders and heroes listed in this chapter, there are some who were clearly not up to the job. We might explain this in karmic terms, saying that the person's attempts to lead or be a star were derailed by a trauma inflicted upon them in a previous incarnation. However, we can also see this as the result of bad choices and of letting ego get ahead of good sense.

This brings us to the one thing that the Sun aspecting the North Node cannot provide. That is a moral code. The Sun seeks attention: it seeks to lead, inspire, and express its solar power. There are no rules imbedded in this archetype as to how this might be accomplished. This is why the people who seem to do the best with these aspects are those who understand the necessity of discipline and firm principles. They also tend to be people who know themselves and recognize their limitations. If you have the Sun aspecting the North Node, you are right in thinking you have been given a gift, but you have also been given a great responsibility. You will never know the full benefits of the former until you accept the burdens of the latter.

CHAPTER 3

The Sun Aspecting
the South Node

*Technical Node—Because the Lunar Nodes are always 180 degrees apart,
an aspect to one is an aspect to both. In distinguishing aspects to the North
Node from aspects to the South Node, I chose the aspects that I regarded as
the strongest. For the South Node, that was the conjunction (0 degrees), the
trine (120 degrees), and the quincunx (150 degrees). The subject of orbs will be
explained in chapter 14.*

There is a difference between the way that the archetype of the Sun functions in the lives of people with the Sun aspecting the North Node and
the way it functions for people when it is aspecting the South Node. What is
this difference? It certainly isn't that people with the Sun aspecting the South
Node lack the ambition and the "look what I can do" solar pride that we
saw with aspects to the North Node. These people possess the same need
to shine. It is the manner in which and the means by which they attempt to
shine that are different. Over and over in this group, we see people whose
success was somehow incomplete. We find leaders without followers and
heroes who inspired the wrong people for the wrong reasons. We also see

people whose accomplishments were compromised by forces beyond their control or by the standards and prejudices of the societies in which they lived.

Putting this in the context of reincarnation, we might assume that what these people suffered was the product of bad karma, that they were repeating unproductive patterns from past lives or that their troubles in this life were recompense for sins committed in a previous incarnation. However, if bad karma is a factor, it certainly isn't an impediment for success and prominence. In terms of pure numbers, the list of celebrities I gathered with the Sun aspecting the South Node was only slightly shorter than my list of famous people with the Sun aspecting the North Node.

Another way of approaching this phenomenon is to see the Sun aspecting the South Node as teaching us about a different side of prominence and success. Writing a best seller or being elected to high office might seem to be the epitome of success, but such accomplishments could also be the starting point for a precipitous fall from grace. If you pay attention, you can learn just as much about yourself and your place in the great scheme of the universe from the latter as you can from the former. Obviously, this is not an easy assignment. No one with the Sun active in their horoscope wants to hear boos or derision from their audience. But there is a lesson to be learned from those rejections and criticisms. It's just not a lesson that most of us are prepared to welcome.

This is not to say that people with the Sun aspecting the South Node can't display the extraordinary self-confidence and star mentality we saw with some of the examples cited with the Sun aspecting the North Node. And yet, overall, that flamboyant egotism is rare among this group. There are no Napoleons, no Mussolinis, here. That may be because people with the Sun aspecting the South Node so often find their way forward blocked and their aims frustrated by serious impediments built into the world in which they were born.

Impediments

In 1558, the fiery Scottish preacher John Knox wrote a book that blasted what he considered to be the greatest abomination of his time: nations ruled by women. It so happened that in that same year, Elizabeth I (who had the Sun quincunx the South Node) took the throne in England while, in Scotland, the sixteen-year-old Mary, Queen of Scots (who had the Sun trine the South Node), was the monarch.

Mary probably paid little attention to the admonitions of John Knox, but his paternalistic rant had dire implications for her reign. A short time later, the young queen was deprived of her throne, imprisoned, and forced to flee her native land. Mary eventually escaped to England, where she was kept under house arrest and eventually beheaded on orders from her cousin, Elizabeth.

Elizabeth fared better. She enjoyed a long and productive reign, but her gender was still an impediment. Unlike male rulers, who were free to sleep with whomever they liked and sire illegitimate children by the score, Elizabeth was forced to remain (at least as far anyone could tell) a virgin.

The impediment facing Elizabeth and Mary was the product of their gender. For Josephine Baker, who had the Sun trine the South Node, and Lena Horne, who had the conjunction, it was their race. Both were talented Black entertainers living in the United States during the era of segregation. Baker fled to Europe, where her race was not an impediment, and her career thrived. Horne remained in the States, but her career as an actress was constrained by the unwillingness of white audiences to accept a Black leading lady.

Despite the impediments they faced, both Josephine Baker and Lena Horne were still able to have successful careers. This is true of many people with the Sun aspecting the South Node. Helen Keller, who had the Sun conjunct the South Node, was able to overcome severe physical impediments with the help of a gifted teacher. Even though Galileo Galilei (who also had the conjunction) was forced by the Inquisition to recant his discoveries with regard to the motion of the planets, his ideas survived and became part of the scientific revolution. Charles Atlas was able to remake his "ninety-pound weakling" body through exercise. Actress Sigourney Weaver was considered too tall to be a leading lady. She became one of the first female action heroines instead.

The impediments that aspects to the South Node seem to place on the exercise of a person's ego can seem overwhelming. They may be imbedded in the society in which you live and accepted as a fact of life by everyone around you. And yet, when the solar archetype is activated in your horoscope, it demands that you challenge these impediments, that you look for a way to assert your ego and display your individuality. You may do this by insisting that the world acknowledge your special talents and abilities, as Josephine Baker and Galileo did. You may insist that the world recognize your power and authority, as did Elizabeth I.

This attitude is not likely to make your life any easier. If you have the Sun aspecting the North Node, these difficulties will only make you stronger. In this case, the solar archetype gives you a greater chance of overcoming those impediments and having the world concede to your specialness. With the Sun aspecting the South Node, however, your path is going to be more difficult. You may feel weighed down by the impediments. You might need to find a helper (as Helen Keller did) or adjust your ambitions. You may have to accept that you are not going to accomplish all your goals. But that doesn't mean that you are giving up your right to shine or that the solar archetype has in any way been defeated.

Shame

Sometimes the obstacle placed before people with the Sun aspecting the South Node of the Moon are not physical or the product of ignorance and prejudice. Sometimes the person with this aspect pursues a course of action that veers away from what is expected by the society in which they live. In some cases, they do things that make them misfits and outsiders or that earn them recrimination and disapproval. They are made to feel ashamed. We saw some of this with Galileo. The great scientist was probably never ashamed of the discoveries he made, but that was what the Church expected of him. Other people in this group faced similar expectations of shame.

Tammy Faye Bakker did not participate in her TV evangelist husband's financial fraud and was ignorant of his sexual peccadillos, and yet she shared his public humiliation when their empire collapsed and Jim was sent to prison. As chief mistress of King Louis XV, Madame de Pompadour became one of the most influential women in France, but to the royals who mingled at the court of Versailles, she remained the King's whore.

Of course, there are some people with the Sun aspecting the South Node who have or had good reason to feel ashamed: people like Lizzie Borden, the terrorist known as Carlos the Jackal, football coach and rapist Jerry Sandusky, guitarist and murderer Sid Vicious, and gangster Lucky Luciano. In the horoscopes of all these people, there are other indicators that create the possibility of violent or aberrant behavior. They do not represent the norm.

When the Sun is aspecting either of the Lunar Nodes, the person is likely to feel a push to stand out and do something extraordinary. This is particularly true when this trait is supported by the rest of the horoscope. People with the Sun aspecting the South Node, unfortunately, are more likely to encounter obstacles in their effort to shine. Some people respond to those impediments by simply finding an easier route to the prominence they seek. Maybe they just don't ask questions that should be asked, or maybe they consciously ignore moral standards that might slow down their advance. They may also come to believe that the extra obstacles they've faced have entitled them to special indulgences. We might blame these lapses on some sort of past life trauma, but, in most cases, it is simply evidence of human weakness, and there is no archetype that can fix that.

Failure

Erwin Rommel's success as a military man was already well established even before World War II. However, the war made him famous. He was called the "desert fox" because of his mastery of mechanized warfare and mobility. Rommel was also a loyal supporter of Adolf Hitler. But when his name was connected to an assassination plot against the Fuhrer in the waning days of the war, the great general was given a choice by the Gestapo: either a long and humiliating show trial, or suicide. Rommel chose suicide.

Rommel had the Sun conjunct the South Node. He enjoyed enormous success for most of his career. He was a star and a hero in Germany. Then, at the very end, he was faced with failure and shame. We find a similar situation in the life of another person with the Sun conjunct the South Node: Amelia Earhart. Earhart completed one daredevil feat after another during the pioneer days of aeronautics. She was portrayed by the press as the heroine of air. And yet, it is her last flight, her failed attempt to circumnavigate the globe, that is most remembered today.

The failures of Rommel and Earhart were sudden and climactic. For other people with the Sun aspecting the South Node, the failure and the shame that came with it lingered. As president, Lyndon Johnson (who had the trine) was able to move groundbreaking legislation through congress, like the Civil Rights Act and Medicare. And yet, the one thing he couldn't do was find a way to "win" the Vietnam War. This was a failure of which President Johnson was constantly reminded, both by antiwar protesters and by daily casualty reports from the field, and it haunted him even after he left the presidency.

Failure is not predestined when the Sun is aspecting the South Node of the Moon. There are many people with this aspect who enjoyed stellar careers without having to suffer through failure and shame. What the solar archetype that comes to us through the South Node brings is an awareness of the fleeting, illusionary nature of success and fame. It shows us the limitations of worldly achievement and how paltry and unsubstantial it appears against the backdrop of the universe. Maybe this is because of a past life experience in which success was achieved and then cruelly taken away. Or maybe it comes out of a deeper awareness of the true purpose of human consciousness and the great mystery that surrounds us all.

Sometimes it takes a shattering crash-and-burn scenario, like the one suffered by Erwin Rommel, to teach us the limitations of our achievements. In other instances, this awareness comes to us in more subtle ways. It could be just a quiet awareness that the applause you're hearing, the money you're making, and the titles you're accumulating don't really matter. You may wonder why these accomplishments, which everyone else seems to think are so important, leave you cold. You might think you're missing something that everyone else sees when, actually, you have sensed something deep and true that so many others choose to ignore.

The Archetype and You

One way of looking at aspects to the South Node is to say that, perhaps because of evil deeds done in a past life, people with these aspects are "fated" never to succeed, or at least never to find satisfaction in their success. Their creative talents and skills are not likely to be fully recognized, and their efforts to seek this recognition may only bring them frustration or, in the worst-case scenario, shame, ridicule, and condemnation. The problem with this theory, besides the fact that it is so absolute and bleak, is that we have several examples of people with these aspects who did succeed, whose talents were recognized, and who weren't cursed with shame, ridicule, or condemnation.

As it is with all the archetypes brought into our lives by aspects to the Nodes, much depends on what else is going on in the horoscope. If the chart has strong indicators of success, these aspects are not going to change that. Instead, they give you a warning: If you identify too closely with your achievements, if you make your self-esteem and ego totally dependent upon them, you will suffer. You will suffer because those successes can be taken away. They can be replaced by failure and shame. Even if this does not happen, your awareness that it could happen will make it difficult for you to fully enjoy and celebrate your accomplishments.

That is the real challenge of the Sun aspecting the North Nodes of the Moon. It is not the risk that you might suffer some dramatic fall from grace (though that is certainly a possibility); it is this basic question about the value and importance of success. In some cases, just the fact that you ask this question can undercut your self-confidence and make it difficult for you to fully express your desire, your will, and your ego. It could ruin your taste for the "rat race" and keep you sitting at the sidelines. However, just because you understand the fleeting nature of the applause doesn't mean you don't desperately want to hear it. Even aspecting the South Node, the solar archetype, with all its ego and thirst for attention, is activated. You may be sitting on the sidelines, but you're probably still waiting for, even expecting, someone to notice your specialness.

More often, though, sitting on the sidelines is not enough for people born with the Sun aspecting the South Node. These folks have to get into the race. Some of you might choose to ignore your misgivings about the value of success. You might think that your success will be different or that your talents and skills are sufficient to overcome those misgivings. There is nothing wrong with this. You may achieve everything you've set out to achieve. But you have to be prepared for the lesson this archetype brings us. It may come to you in a dramatic fashion, or it might be just a quiet recognition that, despite all your work and talent, you missed a very important point.

In chapter 2, we saw several examples of people with the Sun aspecting the North Node for whom things went terribly wrong. Remember Charlie Sheen and Michael Avenatti? However, the people in the North Node group seem to bring trouble upon themselves through their own actions. For people with the Sun aspecting the South Node, more often something they can't control or the actions of other people disrupt their success. Tammy Faye Bakker was brought down by the actions of her husband. Erwin Rommel was probably not conspiring to assassinate Hitler. What keeps you from fulfilling your dreams of success might be bad luck or a matter of being in the wrong place at the wrong time.

Faced with the impediments that this archetype tends to put in your way, you might be tempted to just give up, to cease your striving and accept defeat. This is not generally a good choice. Giving up will only deepen your frustration and further stymie your solar ego. In some cases, giving up could lead to cynicism and sublimated anger. A better ploy is to sit yourself down at the feet of this archetype and learn all it has to teach you about the nature of success, failure, and life in general. These lessons won't be easy. They are likely to change your priorities and cause you to seem out of step with your peers. They may, to some extent, rob you of your competitive edge and hunger for victory. But what you will receive instead is a truth about the value of human accomplishment and the purpose of human life that will allow you to accept whatever comes your way, success or failure, with equanimity and peace of mind.

CHAPTER 4

The Moon Aspecting the
North or South Nodes

The function of the Moon in the horoscope is very different from that of
the Sun. While the Sun initiates and pushes us outward into the world,
the Moon watches and stands ready to pull us back in when any sort of physical, emotional, or psychic danger presents itself. The Moon is reactive. It
responds to what it feels, not to what it sees or thinks. The influence of the
Moon flows through our emotions, our instincts, and the subconscious. We
often don't have any idea what the Moon is doing until a powerful "feeling"
comes over us or we are gripped by motivations that might appear to be irrational and without basis in fact. Understanding the workings of the Moon
can be difficult, but we ignore its warnings at our peril.

The emotional, reactive manner in which the Moon functions means that
people can express that function in very different ways. The way I actualize the Moon in Libra might be completely unlike the way you express that
placement because of differences in our circumstances, our upbringing, our
age, and other factors that might affect our emotional state at that time. The
poetic description of the Moon as ever changing and inconstant has definite
application to the way it functions in the horoscope. Every indicator in a

horoscope can have different meanings depending on various circumstances, but nothing is quite as changeable and difficult to predict as the Moon.

That creates a problem when it comes to naming the archetype that the Moon aspecting the Nodes could represent. Traditionally, the Moon is associated with the Mother. It is also associated with femininity in general, but it shares that characterization with Venus. Mothers and mothering belong to the Moon alone. When the Moon is strongly placed in a horoscope, regardless of the gender of the person, we expect to see these maternal qualities. We expect sensitivity and empathy toward all of humanity, but, in particular, we expect people with a strongly placed Moon to be protective of their loved ones. We expect them to be nurturers and capable of deep emotional bonds.

This is how the Moon functions within the personality, but, as we have seen, the way an archetype functions when it aspects the Lunar Nodes is something else entirely. Instead of strong instincts toward mothering, with aspects between the Moon and the Nodes, we find a desire to be mothered and a vulnerability to the outside world that requires mothering. What we find is the archetype of the Child.

Of course, there are different kinds of children and different ways of embodying this archetype. There is the adorable child we love and cherish. There is the vulnerable child, fearful and defenseless in the cruel world. There is the good child who, in its innocence and openness, shows us the best side of humanity. And there is the bad child, whose selfishness and self-indulgence show the worst of human nature. The archetype of the Child can take on any of these attributes.

The Adorable Child

Since the examples we're using are celebrities, we have to expect that most of them enjoyed a degree of popularity. However, there are some celebrities who take that popularity to a higher level. They are not just liked, they are adored. They don't just have name recognition, they have names that have become iconic, names that elicit an emotional response from us every time we hear them. Names like Harpo Marx and Robin Williams (both of whom had the Moon conjunct the North Node), Princess Diana and Carrie Fisher (both with the Moon conjunct the South Node), Mr. (Fred) Rogers (who had the square), Lucille Ball and Prince (who had the Moon trine the North Node), Dolly Parton (who has the Moon trine the South Node), Marilyn Monroe (who had the Moon quincunx the North Node), and Elvis Presley (who had the Moon quincunx the South Node).

What makes these celebrities so popular? Why do they seem to touch us in such a deep and emotional way? Many of them are or were uniquely talented people, of course. Some of them were also physically beautiful. But the place they hold in our hearts goes far beyond talent or sex appeal. Instead, we are attracted to their essential humanity, that illusive quality that makes us think that we know them even though we don't. We are also drawn to them because we sense that behind their public personas, a vulnerability and a need call out for our love.

The popularity of people like Harpo Marx, Elvis Presley, and Marilyn Monroe has spanned generations. This is not always the case for people with the Moon aspecting the Nodes. Will Rogers (who had the Moon conjunct the South Node) is not well remembered now, but he was one of the most beloved Americans in the entire world during the 1920s and '30s. Rogers began his stage career doing rope tricks, but it was his witty repartee that drew attention. His talent for pithy comments and humorous epigrams on politics and society made Rogers a star on radio and in movies. He also wrote a popular newspaper column. When Rogers died in a plane crash in 1935, the nation mourned.

For a period stretching from the 1930s to the 1950s, Roy Rogers was the King of the Cowboys. He was a successful singer, appeared in scores of movies, and (along with his wife, Dale Evans) starred in radio and TV shows. Roy Rogers's sanitized and sequined version of Western life had its day, but when that day passed, so did much of his popularity. Today, Roy Rogers's iconic status is only evidenced by the many lunch boxes and other collectibles from the 1950s that bear his image.

For other people with these aspects, popularity comes and goes. It might be hard to imagine now, but in his youth, Prince Charles enjoyed the kind of popularity, particularly with young women, generally reserved for rock stars. His ex-sister-in-law, Sarah Ferguson, was cheered by the public when she first entered the royal family. Her informality and lack of pretense were seen as a breath of fresh air. It didn't take long, however, for Fergie to become the object of vicious criticism.

In other instances, the popularity conveyed by this archetype can be specific to a particular group of people. Some people adored conservative radio host Rush Limbaugh, who had the Moon conjunct his North Node. Others have a picture of Che Guevara, who had the same placement, hanging in their room. "Foodies" adore Julia Child, who had the Moon conjunct the South Node, while every aspiring "techie" idolizes Steve Jobs, who had the Moon square the Nodes.

It is not surprising that the popularity that seems to be conveyed by aspects between the Moon and the Nodes can be specific to certain segments of the population. The archetype of the Child gives us the ability to connect with people on deep emotional levels. The people who respond to that connection do so in a subjective way. They can't really explain the connection they feel, and those of us who are in a different place in our emotional lives may have trouble understanding it. Even if the appeal is spread across a mass audience (as it is with people like Marilyn Monroe and Elvis Presley), each fan responds to it in a way that feels specific and personal.

Like most things in life, popularity is what you make of it, and we do have examples of people with the Moon aspecting the Nodes who misused their ability to connect with others in a deeply emotional and personal way. Jim Jones's appeal was limited to a few hundred people and Charles Manson's to a few dozen, and yet their control over those relatively few followers was terrifyingly complete. In chapter 2, I have noted that the archetypes that come to us through aspects to the Nodes do not seem to bring with them a sense of morality. That's something that we have to provide. When we don't, things can go badly. That seems to be particularly true when it is the Moon that is aspecting the Nodes.

The Misbehaving Child

The same children who charm us with their innocence and vulnerability can also drive us crazy with their misbehavior. They whine, complain, grab, yell, and break things. The reason for this, of course, is a lack of impulse control. Children don't see why they shouldn't have what they want when they want it. They don't know about delayed gratification. They don't see danger. They don't care about rules. They will do what they want until some adult stops them.

For people with the Moon aspecting the Nodes, this lack of impulse control can lead to a variety of excesses. For Elvis Presley and Orson Welles, it was primarily food. For Jim Morrison, Kurt Cobain, and several other rock stars, it was primarily drugs. For poet Dylan Thomas and Edgar Allan Poe, it was alcohol. For Bobby Riggs and Pete Rose, it was gambling. For Leopold von Sacher-Masoch (for whom masochism was named) and the Marquis de Sade (for whom sadism was coined), it was a particular variety of sexual play.

In most of these examples, the horoscope shows a tendency toward addiction, usually with Neptune or Jupiter playing a role. Once again, the guest works with what the personality described by the horoscope gives it. However, even people without addiction issues can have problems with these aspects to the Lunar Nodes. We all have had our moments of weakness, occasions when we drop our guard and open the way to impulses that might have otherwise seemed foreign to our personality or character. When the archetype of the Misbehaving Child is active in your horoscope, those moments of infantile self-indulgence can have results that range from embarrassment to disaster.

The Vulnerable Child

Vulnerability is a two-way street. It can help you connect with other people on a deep, emotional level. It can make you attractive, popular, and easy to forgive, no matter how badly you misbehave. But it can also leave you open to the influence of people whose intentions are harmful or misguided. We can see this in the fact that, along with their leader, two of Charles Manson's most well-known female followers, Leslie Van Houten and Patricia Krenwinkel, had aspects between the Moon and the Nodes. The same hidden influencer that made it possible for Manson to connect with his followers made these women especially vulnerable to his uncanny powers of persuasion.

The Child is trusting. The Child is innocent. The Child is often fearful. The Child may also be drawn to strong personalities that exude confidence and promise protection. The fact that some of these stronger personalities might take advantage of the vulnerability of the person with the Moon aspecting the Nodes might seem obvious to us, but, all too often, the Child remains oblivious to this possibility.

When she was still a teenager, Eva Braun, who had the Moon quincunx the North Node, fell in love with Adolf Hitler, who was then just another German politician. Eva complied with Hitler's demand that their relationship remain secret and never wavered in her loyalty to her man. Fifteen years later, Hitler rewarded Eva's devotion by putting a wedding ring on her finger. A few minutes later, he handed her a suicide pill. Brian Wilson of the Beach Boys, with the Moon conjunct the North Node, had absolute faith in the advice given to him by his psychiatrist. That faith put both his music career and his sanity in jeopardy.

Some people with the Moon aspecting the Nodes react to the vulnerability of the Child in a very different way. They see this vulnerability as a weakness that undercuts their pride and their dignity. These are typically people who, for various reasons, feel that they have to be seen by the world as strong, tough, and confident. They often seek to counter the vulnerability that they feel by behaving in a belligerent and violent manner. Their aggressive behavior is essentially a defense mechanism, but that doesn't make it any less damaging to that person's psychic health and to the well-being of the people around them.

There are moments, of course, when we want to see people with these aspects being more defensive and less trusting. However, too much of this defensiveness, too much fear, can deprive these people of the best qualities of this archetype. It can make it difficult for them to be open about their feelings and sympathetic to the feelings of others. It can separate the person from the greatest gift the Child has to offer: the ability to find and celebrate the emotional bonds that unite us all.

This brings us back to the personality described by the rest of the horoscope. It is here that we can learn how the person will respond to this archetype and how well they will be able to balance the dangers of their vulnerability with its advantages. Those who are able to achieve this balance and display their childlike openness without fear and defensiveness often have a special understanding of the vulnerability of their fellow human beings. This can make them excellent counselors and therapists.

The Good Child

There are moments in which children inspire us with their openness, their innocence, and their ability to love unconditionally. There are also times when the archetype of the Child can be inspirational, and people with aspects to the Moon can show surprising selflessness. In these instances, the empathy, the love, the emotional connection that people with these aspects feel is not just with a few individuals or a particular audience, but with the entire world. We don't have a lot of examples of this face of the archetype, but the ones we have are truly remarkable.

Wilhelm Rontgen (who had the Moon conjunct the North Node) discovered X-rays. At the time, his discovery was considered a medical miracle. It could have made Rontgen a rich man. But he decided not to patent his discovery. He gave X-ray technology to the world and asked for nothing in return. Jonas Salk (who had the Moon conjunct the North Node) did the same thing when his laboratory developed the polio vaccine. Marie Curie (who had the Moon conjunct the South Node) never patented the amazing discoveries she made with regard to the medical applications of radiation. Albert Schweitzer (who also had the same conjunction) gave up his career as a minister and a musician to go to medical school so he could establish a hospital in Africa. Bob Geldof (who had the Moon square the Nodes) used his status as a rock star in order to stage famine relief concerts.

What these people show us is not just the best side of this Lunar archetype, but the best of human nature. They also show us the power of the Moon and of human emotion when it is channeled in the right direction. Of course, most people with the Moon aspecting the Nodes have neither the genius nor the resources to develop a lifesaving vaccine or open a hospital, but that doesn't mean you can't aspire to that level of compassion.

The Archetype and You

The thing about celebrity examples is that they tend to represent extremes, which is good for illustrating a point, but somewhat intimidating when you try to apply what they have experienced to your own life. This is particularly the case with the Moon aspecting the Nodes. Among the examples cited in this chapter, we have some of the most beloved and the most hated individuals in human history. This shows us just how inconstant and wide-ranging the influence of the Moon can be. It includes the entire spectrum of human emotion, from the best to the worst.

Seeing the behaviors of the examples cited here in terms of reincarnation is complicated by the fact that there seems to be no difference between what happens when the Moon is aspecting the North Node or the South Node. For the popular examples, both Nodes seem to be equally positive, and for the misbehaving examples, both seem to be equally negative. However, thinking of the Moon's archetype as the Child does raise one interesting point. For most of human history, the chances that any infant would live to become an adult were not good. Many died at birth. Many others died of diseases, accidents, and malnutrition. Some of those children were loved and cherished. Some were abused and brutalized. Some died in the arms of an adoring parent. Others died alone and scared. If we accept that the emotions we felt as we left a past life filter into our present incarnation, then these very different exits, as internalized through the mind of a child, would result in very different behaviors.

As always, other factors in the horoscope play a large role in which face of the Lunar archetype will gain dominance within an individual's personality. The examples with extraordinary popularity typically had placements or aspects that also tended to convey success and popularity, while the horoscope of the Misbehaving Child showed tendencies toward self-indulgence. Another factor is the way the horoscope interacts with the vulnerability provided for by this archetype. Charts that emphasize pride and independence can make it difficult for a person to understand this vulnerability and capitalize on the advantages it presents.

We might assume that this archetype will come into our lives in one guise or another and never change. However, it is probably more common for the Child to show itself in a variety of ways during a person's life. The changeable nature of the Moon flows through this guest, and its attributes shift back and forth. The Vulnerable Child can become the Misbehaving Child if influenced by the wrong type of person, and the Misbehaving Child can become the Adorable Child or even the Good Child when it seeks our forgiveness.

If you have the Moon aspecting one of the Nodes you have to accept this inconsistency. You have to accept that this archetypical visitor will come to you in different forms at different times in your life. What is important is that you avoid taking the different forms of the Child to extremes. A little bit of the Misbehaving Child can spice up your life and make you a fun companion. Too much will get you arrested. The same goes for openness, vulnerability, and even popularity. There are expectations when you are everyone's darling. People only want to see you one way, and given the inconsistence of the Moon, sooner or later, you are going to disappoint them.

However, the biggest challenge that aspects by the Moon to the Lunar Nodes present is the fact that their influence runs through our emotions and our subconscious. This often defies rational explanation. When asked why you abandoned your diet or trusted that shady stranger, all you can do is shrug. Did a memory from a former life when you were a hungry child cry out to you? Did you sense something within that stranger that went beyond their physical appearance and circumstances? The archetype of the Moon provides you with no easy answers to these questions. All it gives you is feelings.

You may have equal difficulty explaining why people react to you in certain ways. Why do people you hardly know pour their hearts to you? Why does the bully always seem to look your way? Why is it that often someone else (probably another bully) jumps up to defend you? With the Moon aspecting the Nodes, you walk through the world as a child, and the people around you may be prone to love you, chastise you, protect you, and, occasionally, ignore you, as they would a child. The fact that you are seeking to make a different impression might seem irrelevant.

These are the kinds of things you may have to learn to live with if you have the Moon aspecting the Lunar Nodes. Doing this gracefully requires a high level of emotional maturity, and even then there are likely to be moments in which you will trust the wrong person or act irresponsibly. Not only do you have to accept these moments, but you also have to learn how to forgive yourself for them. After all, they are essentially evidence of your humanity, the same humanity we all share. This essential humanity is what the Moon and the archetype of the Child really represent. Understanding this will not only help you deal with your own inconsistencies, but also make you more sensitive to and forgiving of the basic humanity of everyone around you.

CHAPTER 5

Mercury Aspecting the North or South Nodes

Mercury could be considered the tagalong of the planets. It's never more than 28 degrees from the Sun. This means that Mercury spends much of the time obscured from our view by the brightness of its huge, gaseous neighbor and that, in the horoscope, it is regularly the same sign and house as the Sun. For this reason, Mercury's influence, particularly when compared to that of the Sun and Moon, is often considered secondary. The Sun and the Moon together make up the essential structure of the personality. What can Mercury add to that?

Plenty, actually. Mercury represents our rational, problem-solving mind. Everything we do, from potty training to computer programing, comes from Mercury's problem-solving function. Mercury also describes how we take in and give out information. It represents our thinking processes, our speech, and our awareness of the world around us. While the Sun and the Moon describe our basic self, Mercury shows us how that "self" deals with the ever-changing, always challenging minutia of living.

There are several different archetypal figures that might be associated with Mercury. The mental acuity and wit of the Jester certainly has a connection with Mercury's symbolism. The planet also has a lot to do with physical dexterity and hand-eye coordination, so maybe the Magician would apply. Its association with travel and dealmaking might make the Merchant a likely candidate. However, the archetype that seems to best represent Mercury is the one for which it was named: the wing-footed deity Mercury, the messenger of the gods.

The Messenger

This brings up important questions: Aren't we all messengers? Don't we all share information, whether it be about the weather, current affairs, or the best dog groomer in town? This is very true. Every horoscope has Mercury placed somewhere, doing its work in one way or another. On top of that, we all have a Third House in our horoscopes, in which we process information about the world close to us, and a Ninth House, in which we talk about the big issues like religion and philosophy. The fact is that gathering and disseminating information is as essential to human nature and the existence of our species as opposable thumbs.

The difference for people with Mercury aspecting the Lunar Nodes is that, when this archetype is active, this basic human function can become the dominant feature of their lives. They become the Messenger with a capital *M*. They have to speak, they have to sing, they have to write books, or blog, or draw pictures, or litter the internet with their likes and retweets. That's because they have messages growing inside them that they must get out into the world. The content of that message might not always be consistent. It also might not seem that important to other people. It might be a message devised by someone other than the Messenger, maybe even by someone completely unknown to the Messenger. All that doesn't matter. All that matters is that the message be delivered.

Putting this in the context of reincarnation, we might assume that a person with Mercury aspecting the Nodes was a messenger in a past life. Maybe they were a shaman, or a traveling minstrel, or a seer. However, it is also possible that the reason these people seem so compelled to speak out in this life is because they were silenced in past lives. Due to their social status, religious traditions, or gender, they were not allowed to say the things that needed to be said, and those unspoken messages dried up and died within their souls. That's why they have made it their mission in this life to not let that happen, to say what's on their minds and to be heard.

The Storyteller

The most common type of Messenger we see, at least among our celebrity examples, is the Storyteller. Storytellers are people who feel compelled to relate to others, or to the entire world, their personal story or the stories of other people with whom the Storytellers can identify. Storytellers predominate among our famous examples because human societies have always valued a good storyteller. It isn't just about entertainment. The Storyteller allows us to experience, in an indirect and innocuous way, the lives of people who are not like us. Sometimes, those lives are better than ours. Sometimes they're worse. In either case, they allow us to forget the immediate concerns of our own lives, at least for a while.

In ages past, it was the singer with his lyre who told the stories, or the tribal elder who recited the history of the clan to the next generation. In our own time, Storytellers can tell their stories in a variety of ways. However, the medium most closely associated with the Storyteller's art is the written word, and, as you might expect, there are a lot of great writers with these aspects. This is not to say that you have to have an aspect between Mercury and the Nodes in order to be a great writer. There are also many great writers who don't have these aspects. But the ones who do seem to tell stories that have an extra edge, stories that work their way into the seams of human consciousness and endure.

Robert Louis Stevenson, who had Mercury square the Nodes, gave us Dr. Jekyll and Mr. Hyde. Victor Hugo, with Mercury conjunct the North Node, gave us the Hunchback of Notre-Dame. Margaret Mitchell, who also had Mercury conjunct the North Node, gave us Scarlett O'Hara. F. Scott Fitzgerald, who had Mercury trine the North Node, gave us Gatsby. Gustave Flaubert, also with the square, gave us Madame Bovary. Lewis Carroll and Louisa May Alcott, both with Mercury quincunx the North Node, gave us Alice and

Josephine March. H. P. Lovecraft, with Mercury square the Nodes, introduced Cthulhu into our nightmares.

These examples illustrate one of the special things about storytellers with Mercury aspecting the Nodes: characters and ideas from the stories they tell often rise above mere entertainment or even literature and hit a societal nerve. They become a part of our language and our culture. You may have never read Samuel Taylor Coleridge's "The Rime of the Ancient Mariner," but when you hear the phrase "It's like an albatross around his neck," you know exactly what that means.

Other authors with Mercury aspecting the Nodes used fiction to make a political or social statement. Along with *The Hunchback of Notre-Dame*, Victor Hugo produced *Les Misérables*, a timeless indictment of social injustice. Frank Herbert, who also had Mercury conjunct the North Node, expressed his real-life concerns about sustainable living and taking care of our environment through his classic science fiction novel *Dune*. Erica Jong, with Mercury conjunct the South Node, used her novels to express her own brand of feminism. In *La Comédie humaine*, Honoré de Balzac wove a series of over ninety novels and short stories into a single narrative in which he sought to create a definitive picture of his times and society.

Of course, you don't have to rely on the written word in order to tell a story. Creative people of all sorts are born with Mercury aspecting the Nodes, and they find different ways to tell their story. The French painter Henri Rousseau, who had Mercury on his South Node, gave us images of far-off lands, arid deserts, and dense jungles. Rousseau had no firsthand knowledge of these places, but that didn't stop him from drawing these exotic locales in his highly imaginative and evocative paintings. Steven Spielberg, who has Mercury conjunct the South Node, and Peter Jackson, who has Mercury trine the South Node, used the magic of movies to tell their stories. Bruce Springsteen, who has Mercury conjunct the South Node, and Mick Jagger, with Mercury trine the North Node, used the lyrics of popular songs. George Gershwin, with Mercury trine the North Node, wrote an opera. Great storytellers find a way to tell their story, and, regardless of the medium they choose, the power of their story will always shine through.

Even if you don't want to write things down and you can't draw or make movies, you can still tell stories. The most distinguishing feature of people with Mercury aspecting the Lunar Nodes is not outstanding talent, but the compulsion to forge their experiences or the experiences of others into a narrative. Maybe that narrative never goes any farther than a story told at the dinner table after work or over a beer or a cup of coffee with a friend. For the person with these aspects, the question isn't how many people hear their story, it is how well it is told.

The Truth-Teller

Another manifestation of the Messenger we often see is the Truth-Teller. These are people who feel compelled to teach and inform us. Their message is less dependent on personal experience and more on factual information. These Messengers speak to us with a greater sense of urgency than the Storytellers. They have facts, opinions, and observations they must share. This doesn't mean that the Truth-Teller is invariably right. The truth is always subject to the biases of the teller. But there can be no doubt that Truth-Tellers believe in what they are saying.

Al Gore, who has Mercury trine his South Node, is an example of this kind of Truth-Teller. He has made it his mission to tell people about climate change. The French oceanographer Jacques Cousteau, who had Mercury conjunct his North Node, devoted his life to informing the world about the wonders of the sea. Betty Friedan (with Mercury trine the North Node) wrote *The Feminine Mystique* and helped start the modern feminist movement. Journalist Ronan Farrow (with Mercury square the Nodes) revealed the crimes of Harvey Weinstein and helped start the Me Too movement.

Not all Truth-Tellers need to write a book or stand at a podium to share their truth. Rosa Parks (who had Mercury trine the South Node) delivered a powerful message by simply refusing to move to the back of the bus. The French poet Arthur Rimbaud (with Mercury conjunct the South Node) is probably better known for his wild and disreputable lifestyle than anything he wrote. Che Guevara delivered his message by helping start a revolution. Anton LaVey expressed his opinion of the social mores of his time by staging satanic rituals. Actions often speak louder than words, and some people with Mercury aspecting the Nodes make ample use of this axiom.

As I said, Truth-Tellers tend to come to us with biases and agendas. There is no mistaking the liberal agenda behind the documentaries of Michael Moore (who has Mercury square the Nodes). Likewise, the conservative agenda of Rupert Murdoch (who has Mercury quincunx the South Node) is broadcast daily on Fox News. Feminists who lined up behind the agenda put forth by Betty Friedan were not so quick to accept the radical, anti-male agenda of Andrea Dworkin (who had Mercury trine the North Node). Nor were many of them ready to sign on to the pro-sex, anti-censorship agenda put forth by porn stars Nina Hartley and Annie Sprinkle (both of whom had Mercury conjunct the South Node).

Some messages are controversial. Others are absolutely toxic. As Hitler's Minister of Propaganda, Joseph Goebbels (who had Mercury square the Nodes) indoctrinated the German public with a constant stream of anti-Semitic literature and images that convinced them that the denigration, imprisonment, and, ultimately, murder of six million Jews would save their country. Around the same time, a former journalist named Benito Mussolini (who had both the Sun and Mercury square the Nodes) was convincing the Italian public that he was making Italy into a world power when, in fact, he was leading them toward a devastating defeat. When John Hinckley Jr., who had Mercury conjunct the South Node, shot President Ronald Reagan, he thought he was sending a message to a certain film star.

Not every person with Mercury aspecting the Nodes makes being a Truth-Teller a full-time job. Bobby Fischer, who had Mercury conjunct the South Node, became famous in his youth as America's chess champion, but his later years were marred by anti-American and anti-Semitic statements that eventually forced him to leave the United States and live in exile in Iceland. Jim Carrey, with Mercury conjunct the South Node, has delighted audiences for years as a comedian and actor, but more recently he has become a painter who uses garish images to express his political opinions. Orson Scott Card, who has Mercury conjunct the South Node, is known to science fiction fans as the author of the award-winning novel *Ender's Game*. However, he is also a devout follower of the Church of Jesus Christ of Latter-Day Saints and a vocal opponent of homosexuality and gay marriage.

The messages brought to us by the Truth-Tellers are not always divisive or controversial. However, when you are convinced that you have a truth to tell, it's hard not to be insistent. Even if your message is about cake recipes or orthopedic shoes, a certain sense of urgency is apt to color your explanations. Too much of this can sour relationships and cause people to walk the other way when they see you coming. The thing that the Truth-Teller has to remember is that the truth you are bringing to the world is *your* truth. That's why you feel so impelled to tell it, but it is also a reason why some people might not be interested in hearing it.

The Failed Messenger

For people with Mercury aspecting the Nodes, whether they are Storytellers or Truth-Tellers or some combination of the two, the most important thing is having something worthwhile to say. That doesn't mean the message has to be particularly important, but it does mean that you have to have given it some thought. You need to understand the meaning of your message and its relevance to the people to whom you are delivering it. A garbled or inconsistent message isn't just a danger to your reputation, it can inspire you or other people to take actions that are unwise and destructive. Flaws in your message can make it easier for it to be misconstrued, twisted, and blown out of proportion. It can turn an innocent story into an insult or a dark insinuation. It can turn your truth into a lie.

Mercury is also associated with our intellectual processes, our ability to think things through in an orderly fashion. The Failed Messenger is someone who is not making the proper use of that side of Mercury. It is someone whose narrative is poorly formed and whose truth is flimsy and unsubstantiated. Such Messengers might appear confused and unbalanced, but that doesn't mean that they don't totally believe in the relevance and truth of their message. The Failed Messenger can still be persuasive and, therefore, dangerous to us all.

Exceptions

The degree to which you respond to any planet aspecting the Nodes of the Moon depends on what's already going on in the rest of your horoscope. The archetype is like a visitor to your horoscope. Its influence is filtered by what's already there. This is especially true with Mercury aspecting the Nodes of the Moon. The Messenger requires a particular kind of mind. It requires focus and clarity. A mind that is clouded by ambition and avarice, or by addiction and self-indulgence, or by emotional or intellectual instability, is typically incapable of that kind of focus. Such minds provide a poor ground for either stories or truths to form, and when the message is unformed, the Messenger is silent.

The Archetype and You

There is no pecking order when it comes to these archetypical figures, but if there were one, you might think that the Sun is at the head. After all, if you have the Sun aspecting the North Node of the Moon, you've come into this life with the expectation of being a Leader, a Hero, or a Star. What could be more important than that? The answer to that question might be Mercury. While the influence of a Star, Hero, or Leader is often situational and temporary, a well-told story or a great truth can resonate across generations. It can give strength to the weak and courage to the meek. That's why having Mercury aspecting the Nodes in your horoscope is not something to be taken lightly. The messages that have been seeded into your consciousness might have waited centuries to be spoken aloud. You have a sacred duty to get it right.

With this aspect, it isn't just the basic personality described by the rest of your horoscope that determines how the archetype of the Messenger will speak. Your level of education and mental acuity are also important factors. People with these aspects have a special responsibility to educate themselves and train their minds. You have to be able to properly sort information, to separate the crucial from the trivial and the true from the false. And it's not just the facts that you need to know. You also need some understanding of human nature and of the type of people who make up your audience. Other people might be able to get away with being intellectually lazy. Other people might do fine with a narrow and specific frame of reference. People with these aspects can't. This archetype demands a mind that is both sharp and well rounded. Without this, your message will falter.

As some of the examples cited in this chapter demonstrate, it is very easy for people with these aspects who are morally misguided to get themselves into trouble, but even knowledgeable, well-meaning Messengers can end up giving out mixed messages. The Hungarian physicist Leo Szilard (who had Mercury conjunct the North Node) was instrumental in convincing the Allies during World War II that they had to develop an atomic bomb before Hitler built one. However, once the United States had the bomb, Szilard led the fight against its use. The Nazis had been defeated by this point, and Szilard feared what would happen once the world witnessed the destructive potential of the weapon he had helped build.

Situations change and new information becomes available. The person with Mercury aspecting Nodes of the Moon has to be able to accommodate these changes. This can be a challenge for some of you. Stubbornness, pride, and a lack of mental flexibility can make it difficult for you to change your message. However, this is something else this archetype demands. Keeping your message up to date and relevant is part of the responsibility of the Messenger.

As with all these archetypical guests, the Messenger can appear at certain times in our life and fade into the background during others. For Bobby Fischer and Jim Carrey, the need to take on the role of Messenger came later in life. For others, it came early. Steven Spielberg made his first film at fifteen. Bruce Springsteen decided that he was going to be a rock star when he was in the third grade. Arthur Rimbaud had written all the poetry he needed to write by the time he was twenty-one. The Messenger doesn't require a place in the entirety of your life. All it needs is enough time to get its message out.

However, even when the Messenger is dormant in your life, it will have its influence. It will cause you to perk up your ears when you hear someone relating an interesting story and to log away facts and figures that support your opinions. You will still feel the urge to form this information into narratives or arguments and expositions even when the Messenger within you seems to be asleep. This will be a factor in the way you think and way you perceive the world. It's not that you are planning to write the great American novel or run for public office. You're just laying the groundwork for the day when the Messenger taps you on the shoulder and tells you that it's time to speak out.

CHAPTER 6

Venus Aspecting the North or South Nodes

Venus is the brightest object in the sky after the Sun and Moon and has been a central feature in the astrology of several cultures. Typically, in Western astrology, it is associated with beauty, comfort, and social grace. However, when Venus is aspecting the Nodes of the Moon, this archetype goes far beyond these rather shallow attributes. Here, Venus represents the power of the Divine Feminine.

We tend to think of the feminine as the opposite of the so-called masculine qualities represented by the Sun and Mars. These masculine qualities are supposed to be active while the feminine is passive. However, the archetype of the feminine is by no means a blushing damsel in distress. It can also be active. It's just that the activity of the feminine is more about creating consensus than conquest. The feminine socializes the ego of the Sun and makes the braggadocio of Mars less about "me" and more about "we." The archetype of the feminine represents a force that goes beyond the designations of gender. It is a power that lives in every human soul, and it is particularly influential and relevant to those of us who have Venus aspecting the Nodes of the Moon.

Mothers

The way this power is expressed can be different for men than for women. In the lives of men, the influence of the Venus archetype is often projected onto a woman in that man's life, typically a strong woman. In many cases, that significant role is filled by the man's mother.

When comedian Milton Berle (who had Venus conjunct the North Node) began his career in Vaudeville, he was still a child, and his mother was there to protect and guide him. As Berle grew older, his mother's influence continued, and it spread to his personal life. She kept a careful eye on the girls he dated, and if any of them seemed likely to take his mother's place as the most important woman in Milton's life, Mrs. Berle found ways to put an end to the relationship.

In other instances, the mother in question was less overbearing, but still a strong woman. Frank Sinatra (who had Venus quincunx the South Node) and Presidents Franklin Roosevelt (with Venus quincunx the North Node) and Jimmy Carter (with Venus conjunct the North Node) all benefited from the influence of a strong-willed mother. For other men with Venus aspecting the Nodes, the connection with their mother was less direct. Winston Churchill (with Venus trine the North Node) adored his mother, but she was a distant ideal with little time to devote to her son. Instead, Churchill developed a close bond with the nanny who gave him the attention and affection that his mother couldn't. Truman Capote had Venus conjunct the North Node. His mother left him to be raised by relatives when he was four. By the time she returned to take charge of the boy five years later, he had formed a close bond with an elderly female relative he called Sook. Lord Byron (with Venus trine the South Node) was openly antagonistic toward his alcoholic mother, but, with his fortune-seeking father mostly absent, she was the only parent he knew.

The influence the mother has on the man with Venus conjunct the Nodes can vary. So can the effect that influence has on his behavior. Deep psychological issues involving their relationships with their mothers was likely a factor in the chronic womanizing of both Milton Berle and Lord George Byron. Truman Capote was equally promiscuous with men. Franklin Roosevelt wasn't necessarily promiscuous, but he was unfaithful to his wife. On the other hand, Winston Churchill and Jimmy Carter both enjoyed long and happy marriages. As we've seen in previous chapters, the influence of this guest is dependent upon what is going on in the horoscope as a whole. Milton Berle and Lord Byron were dealing with a second archetypical visitor. Both also had the Moon aspecting the Nodes, adding tendencies toward emotional vulnerability and self-indulgence.

Wives and Lovers

Franklin Roosevelt was certainly influenced by his strong-willed and doting mother, but the most remarkable relationship in his life was with his wife, Eleanor. This is the other tendency that seems to come with Venus aspecting the Nodes. Even men who were not overly influenced by their mothers typically find their way into singular partnerships with the women who become their wives and lovers. These women, in one way or another, become a major force in the man's life.

Rudolph Valentino's wife, Natacha Rambova, helped him craft the image that would make him a star in silent movies and the first male sex symbol. Tom Arnold is another actor whose career was launched by the woman who was his wife at the time. When James Joyce met Nora Barnacle, he found his muse. The same could be said for the wives of painter Pierre Bonnard and poet Robert Graves. Michael J. Fox's wife helped him deal with the devastating effects of Parkinson's disease. David Crosby's wife helped him survive drug addiction and a prison sentence. For a man with Venus aspecting the Node, the woman he takes as his partner in life often assumes a role far beyond what is typical for a wife or lover.

Sometimes the importance of the relationship that represents this archetype is not immediately apparent. Enrico Fermi didn't need much help from his wife to become the most celebrated physicist in Italy during the 1930s. His work on nuclear physics earned him a Nobel Prize in 1938. However, Fermi was aware that Italy's fascist government was beginning a crackdown on Jews in that country. This mattered a great deal to Fermi, because his wife was Jewish. So, when Fermi went to Stockholm to claim his Nobel, he took a detour on the way home and fled with his wife and family to the United States. Fermi's decision not only protected his wife from persecution, but also changed the course of his life. It led to the scientist becoming a leader in the development of the atomic bomb for the Allies during World War II.

The young Henry VIII of England had no choice in the first woman he married. The politics of the time dictated that he be wed to his dead brother's widow, Catherine of Aragon. But as Henry got older, his affection for Catherine waned, and her failure to produce a male heir made their marriage a political liability. Henry's decision to end his marriage to Catherine and look elsewhere for his feminine ideal became the most decisive act of his long reign and completely rewrote the history of the country he ruled.

It might be said that men with Venus aspecting the Nodes see in the flesh-and-blood women they love an embodiment of their notion of the feminine archetype, and that this raises the way in which they relate to those women to a higher, almost mystical level. In many cases, this seems to be so, but it is not always a good thing. When Elvis Presley met the pretty teenager who would eventually become his bride, he immediately began to remake her into his notion of the "perfect" woman. He chose her clothes, her makeup, and her hairstyle and attempted to control her life. Eventually, Priscilla Presley grew up and began to assert her individuality. Her decision to divorce Presley was a blow from which the "king" never recovered.

Presley's plight illustrates an important point. Just because a man with Venus aspecting the Nodes finds his feminine ideal, that does not guarantee that he will be able to hold on to her. Nor does it mean the relationship will be blessed with peace and harmony. Singer Bobby Brown, who has Venus conjunct the North Node, found this out when he married Whitney Houston. A more tragic example of this truth was the marriage of O. J. Simpson (who has Venus quincunx the South Node) and Nicole Brown Simpson. Having Venus aspecting the Nodes doesn't necessarily make finding love easier, particularly when the rest of the chart says otherwise.

Of course, there is another way of looking at these relationships. We could say that the women who enter the lives of men with these aspects—as mothers, wives, lovers, and otherwise—are the reincarnation of women with whom these men have unfinished business from past lives. We could also say that the ups and downs of these relationships are the product of karmic debts the two people owe one another. Certainly, there is room for these theories. However, when we consider women with these aspects to the Nodes, the story is completely different.

The Power of the Feminine

It is an unfortunate fact of life in our paternalistic society that, of all the examples I've gathered of famous people with Venus aspecting the Nodes, less than a fourth were women. It is interesting, however, that this relatively small sample contains three noted feminists: Gloria Steinem, with Venus conjunct the North Node; Betty Friedan, with Venus quincunx the North Node; and Alva Belmont (who held suffragette meetings in her mansion in Newport, Rhode Island, during the early twentieth century), also with Venus conjunct the North Node.

We also have women in this group who advanced the feminist cause by just being exceptionally good at what they did, such as tennis stars Billie Jean King and Venus Williams and dancer Martha Graham. We have leaders like Margaret Thatcher, and we have women with phenomenal courage, such as Sophie Scholl, the German teenager who spoke out against Hitler at the height of his power and was executed as a traitor. The defining characteristic of these women with Venus aspecting the Nodes is not "femininity." It is strength. Of course, strength in a woman's personality is not always viewed in the same way as it is in a man's, so some of our examples with Venus aspecting the Lunar Nodes, like Margaret Thatcher and reality star Omarosa Manigault, have been called abrasive and callous. What the Divine Feminine brings out in the personality will vary with each person and each horoscope, but it need not be dainty, accommodating, or polite.

What these examples show us is that the feminine archetype can be a source of extraordinary power. When that archetype is fully activated in a woman's character, it gives that individual special access to that power. Sometimes exercising that power means becoming a standout athlete or a great artist. Sometimes it means leading a band or writing poetry. However, that power could also be exercised through activities that don't typically lead to celebrity. The strength of the feminine is an asset in any walk of life, from raising children to leading a country.

Finding your way to the power of the feminine is not always easy. Many women struggle to actualize the strength that is hidden within this archetype. Cher Bono (with Venus conjunct the North Node) and Tina Turner (with Venus trine the South Node) had to first break away from controlling husbands. Katie Couric (with Venus quincunx the North Node) had to fight her way up the ladder of television news personalities to become the first female news anchor for a major network. The Mexican painter Frida Kahlo (also with Venus quincunx the North Node) spent most of her life living in the substantial shadow of her mural-painting husband, Diego Rivera. While Rivera covered walls with depictions of the great societal struggle of workers against capitalists, Kahlo's paintings were considered too personal and too "feminine" to be significant. It was only toward the end of her life that the scales of the art world had shifted, and Frida's powerful and intensely subjective works were given the attention they deserved.

Every woman's journey toward the feminine archetype is different. While some seem to move easily into this role, others only find it after a significant struggle. Some may never find it at all. As always, much depends on what else is going on in the horoscope. Some charts are simply better equipped for this journey than others. For example, Margaret Thatcher had the strength and determination of Scorpio Ascendant and a Leo Moon going for her. Katie Couric was helped by her ambitious Capricorn Sun sign and the fact that she had Mercury (the Messenger) trine the North Node of the Moon. The means of fulfilling this archetype are always going to be different in different charts.

Beauty and Sex

If we were thinking of Venus's aspects to the Nodes of the Moon in terms of personal attributes, we might look for physical beauty and sex appeal in our examples. Certainly, we would find some. Among the men with Venus aspecting the Lunar Nodes, we have Rudolph Valentino, Marlon Brando, Marcello Mastroianni, and Elvis Presley—all men who were once celebrated for their looks. Among the women, there are Cameron Diaz, Angelina Jolie, Britney Spears, and Tina Turner. However, any collection of celebrities is going to feature a lot of people from the performing arts, like actors and actresses, and these people are typically a little better looking than the rest of us. The fact is that there are just as many of these beautiful people with Mercury and the Moon aspecting the Nodes. When it comes to aspects to the Nodes of the Moon, Venus's traditional connection to physical beauty does not seem all that important.

However, even though the archetype of Venus, as it functions in aspects to the Nodes, is not really about physical beauty or sexiness, it does have some interesting connections with sex in general. This is something we see only in a select grouping of these examples, but it is still rather remarkable.

It so happens that three great Victorian researchers in the area of human sexuality were born with Venus aspecting the Nodes: Sigmund Freud, with Venus conjunct the North Node; Richard von Krafft-Ebing, with Venus conjunct the South Node; and Havelock Ellis, with Venus trine the South Node. Freud, of course, is famous for establishing the link between sex and the subconscious. Krafft-Ebing wrote *Sexual Psychopathy*, which, at one time, was considered the last word on the classification of sexual behavior. Havelock Ellis was a prim British doctor who wrote the first medical text on "inversion," or homosexuality. It is likely that Ellis's interest in the subject was spurred by the lesbian inclinations of his wife.

As we've seen from other examples, there is a tendency for men with Venus aspecting the Nodes to be attracted to powerful women. However, in the case of these three men, that attraction seems to have also been toward sexuality as a subject. And they weren't alone. While Freud, Krafft-Ebing, and Ellis all studied sexuality from a scientific point of view, the work of British explorer Sir Richard Burton was more anecdotal and literary. Burton became a notorious figure during the Victorian era because of his writings on sexual practices in Asia and Africa and his translation of the *Kama Sutra*.

The intertwinement of the feminine and sexuality seems to also be a factor for some of our female examples. These are women like Stormy Daniels and reality TV star Anna Nicole Smith, who used their sexuality as a means of making a living. It could be said that these women were also using the power of the feminine, just in a different way than Gloria Steinem or Margaret Thatcher. We could certainly debate whether this was the best use of that power, but, again, every person with Venus aspecting the Nodes has to find their own way to this archetype.

In Between

When we talk about gender issues, we have to also consider those people who don't fit into either side of the biological divide. Sexuality is a spectrum, and people find happiness in various places on that spectrum. For people who don't conform to the traditional, binary divisions of gender, the influence of this guest becomes complex. Once again, everyone has to find their own way to this archetype. For Truman Capote, the feminine seems to have come to him in the form of the elderly relative who raised him. For Gertrude Stein, it was her lifelong partner, Alice B. Toklas. One man among our examples, Harris Glenn Milstead (better known as Divine), spent most of his professional life performing as a woman. One woman, who went by the name Billy Tipton, spent both her professional life (as a jazz musician) and her personal life (through four marriages) as a man.

As we have seen, men and women deal with the influence of this archetype in very different ways. For those in between, it becomes a matter of what else is going on in your horoscope and the way in which you express your gender identity. The manner in which you express the power of the feminine may have nothing to do with your gender at birth.

The Archetype and You

If you have Venus aspecting one of the Nodes of the Moon in your chart, you need to pay particular attention to the way in which you relate to the women in your life. This is true regardless of the gender with which you identify. Some of those women, or perhaps just one of them, is likely to represent to you the essential archetype of the feminine, and your relationship with that woman may have less to do with her character than with the way in which you have related to the feminine through a hundred lifetimes. It is part of a greater mystery, and how you react to that mystery can have deep, karmic implications.

If you're a woman with these aspects, you will be more prone to use these special women as examples, or perhaps as negative examples, who will help you as you aspire toward making the power of the eternal feminine a part of your own life. If you're a man, on the other hand, you will be more prone to project the qualities and mysteries of the feminine onto the important women in your life. If you don't feel that you fit into either of these gender-based categories, you may use either approach, or some combination of the two. The point of these aspects is not the means by which you identify with the Divine Feminine; it is the fact that, someway, somehow, you must.

As was pointed out at the beginning of this chapter, the feminine as an archetype supersedes the purely biological concerns of gender. It is a power unto itself, separate from the power of the Sun and the attributes of the other archetypes and equal to them all. It is a power necessary to everyone who seeks to live in a civilized society in which beauty and fairness have value. People with Venus aspecting the Nodes of the Moon have a special connection to that power. This doesn't mean that they have to always play nice. It just means that, for these people, the rough, egoic power of the masculine has been answered, and to some degree subdued, by the more refined and less self-centered power of the feminine.

Through the centuries, the power of the feminine has been denigrated and ridiculed and feared. These attitudes have persisted into our own time, and they may play a part in how you relate to this archetype. Men with these aspects might see the influence of this guest as encroaching on masculine strength and independence. Different men at different times have reacted to this fear in various ways. For example, it could be said that the whole of Freudianism (Sigmund Freud had Venus conjunct the North Node) is one man's complaint against the power of the feminine as it comes to us through our mothers.

Men with these aspects who adopt such attitudes are likely to have significant difficulties in their relationship with women and with the feminine as it exists in their own souls. Women can have similar difficulties if they have internalized a negative characterization of the feminine. The same applies to those who fall somewhere in between. Aspects by Venus to the Nodes require that you acknowledge and address these prejudices. Otherwise, your way to the feminine will be a long uphill climb.

In terms of reincarnation, the theory is that Venus aspecting the Nodes of the Moon indicates either that you were a woman in a past life or have unfinished business with a woman, or with women in general. As with most things involving reincarnation, it is impossible to confirm or deny this theory. However, we can propose an alternative. Instead of representing a particular gender, let's say that having Venus aspecting the Nodes represents a hiccup in the way in which you related to the archetype of the feminine in previous lives. Maybe you were a male misogynist who denigrated women. Maybe you were a woman who felt cheated by her gender. Maybe you've been different versions of both through a long string of lifetimes. Now is the time to put that struggle behind you. Now is the time to see the issues of femininity and masculinity as part of the greater mystery of human consciousness.

CHAPTER 7

Mars Aspecting the
North or South Nodes

M ars aspecting the Nodes presents us with a special situation because, unlike Venus or Mercury, Mars is considered a "malefic" planet. That is to say that ancient astrologers considered Mars always to be a bad influence, bringing into play anger, violence, and destruction. After all, it's named after the god of war. Though modern astrologers favor a more balanced view of this maligned planet, some of this old negativity still clings to how Mars is read in a horoscope. It is still associated with aggressiveness and acting too quickly or with too much force.

The modern reading, however, gives Mars some positive qualities as well. It is the planet of action, energy, and getting things done. It's still all about fighting, but it's fighting with a purpose. It's fighting to protect your loved ones, your property, and yourself. It's fighting for a cause or a principle. It's fighting to make a living and climb the ladder of success. This fighting spirit is one reason why only my celebrity examples with the Moon aspecting the Nodes (popularity) outnumber the examples I have with Mars. Having Mars aspecting your Lunar Nodes might not be a guarantee of success, but it certainly doesn't hurt.

The Warrior

There's a saying that goes, "Be kind, for everyone you meet is fighting a hard battle." That's good advice for dealing with humanity in general, but it is particularly applicable to people with Mars aspecting the Nodes of the Moon. The archetype that these aspects bring into our lives seems to be a cross between an angry drill sergeant and the hyperactive fitness instructor shouting at you from the screen on your exercise bike. The messages are clear: "Get going!" "Fight through the pain!" "Win, win, win!" It is a call to our inner strength, our courage, and our will. It is a call to the Warrior within us.

Obviously, what we're talking about here is not an actual warrior, but it can be. One example of this is Ulysses S. Grant, who had Mars conjunct the North Node. As a civilian, Grant seemed to be a man without a purpose. He tried several different occupations and failed at them all. However, when the Civil War began, Grant found his calling, and the Warrior within him stepped forward.

Before he entered politics, George H. W. Bush, who had Mars conjunct the North Node, was a fighter pilot and a war hero during World War II. This Warrior spirit reemerged many years later during Bush's presidency when he ordered US forces to invade Panama and oversaw the first Gulf War. Timothy McVeigh, who had Mars quincunx the South Node, fought in that war and served with distinction. When he got home, however, McVeigh started another war, this time with the US government.

Obviously, George Bush and Timothy McVeigh had very different experiences with this archetype. Part of this is explained by differences in their background, class, and generation, and part of it is explained by differences in their horoscopes. And yet, despite these differences, Bush and McVeigh were alike in that playing the role of the Warrior represented a crucial turning point in their lives.

You don't have to be a soldier to play this role. Angela Davis has been fighting against racism and capitalist oppression all her life. At one point, Davis's fight with the US justice system got her to the top of the FBI's Most Wanted list. Davis has Mars trine her North Node. Another Black activist who took a combative approach to the struggle against racism is Stokely Carmichael, who has Mars conjunct the South Node. Also with Mars conjunct the South Node, we have Louis Farrakhan, who, as leader of a faction of the Black Muslims, is noted for his belligerent and divisive remarks.

Another Warrior who never needed to wear a uniform is Ralph Nader, who has spent his life fighting corporate greed. Julian Assange, with Mars conjunct the North Node, has picked fights with a variety of institutions, including banks, corporations, the Democratic Party, and the US government. Friedrich Engels, with Mars square the Nodes, devoted his life to overthrowing the capitalist system. Alfred Kinsey devoted his to battling conventional misconceptions about sexuality. Martin Luther took on the Catholic Church in the sixteenth century. Kate Millett took on the patriarchal establishment in the twentieth.

In some ways, the actions of the folks listed above sound like a description you might see for people with Mars prominent in the horoscope by aspect or placement. The fact is that some of the examples used here do have Mars emphasized in this way. However, having Mars aspecting one of the Nodes is different from having it prominent in your horoscope. The influence of this archetype often seems to function on a separate plane than that of the personality. For example, during the first few years after he finished law school, Ralph Nader was a young man who seemed to have no direction. Then Nader discovered that American car manufactures were putting out vehicles they knew were unsafe, and he took up the fight to change the way those corporations did business. That fight set Ralph Nader on a course he would follow for the rest of his life.

Another man whose life was given purpose by the Warrior was Adolf Hitler, who had Mars trine the South Node. Prior to World War I, Hitler was a failed artist who eked out a living painting bad watercolors of Viennese tourist sights. Then the Warrior came into his life. Hitler's time as a soldier defined him in much the same way as Nader's fight with General Motors defined his life. When World War I ended, Hitler found new enemies and new ways to fight, but the archetype of the Warrior continued to be the driving force in his life.

For some people, the influence of the Warrior and war is less direct. Audrey Hepburn (with Mars trine the South Node) was trapped with her mother in German-occupied Holland when World War II began. Before the war, the teenage Hepburn was studying ballet and had dreams of becoming a ballerina, but the severe deprivation she suffered during the war years left the youngster physically incapable of the rigors of that art. Unable to pursue her dream, young Audrey decided to try acting instead.

Generally speaking, humans are programed to take the path of least resistance. It is often only through extraordinary circumstances that we are persuaded to step outside that path. Mars represents the challenge, the drive, and, in some cases, the rage that allow us to not only march forward against the wind, but also to enjoy the process. For people with Mars prominent in their horoscope, this is a natural tendency. For people with Mars aspecting the Nodes, however, the influence of the Warrior comes from somewhere else. That might be a memory from a past life. It might be that you have been marked for this role by some agency of fate. In either case, your life will in some way be radically changed by combat.

In the course of all this fighting, you may discover qualities within yourself that you never knew you had, such as courage, determination, and resilience. You might also feel that both your outer and inner peace have been ambushed and stolen from you. All of this is dependent on factors in your horoscope. Some of us are better prepared for the role of Warrior than others. For every person with these aspects who delights in the call to battle, there is another who resists and longs for the fighting to stop.

Competition

Whether you're fighting for your country or fighting city hall, warfare is only one way in which the archetype of the Warrior can impact our lives. For many people with Mars aspecting the Nodes of the Moon, it's more about the struggle to make a living. It's about fighting to get ahead in the world. It's about creating a better life for you and your family. It's about something called competition, and this archetype knows all about it.

This is another instance when using a database of celebrities can be a liability. Celebrities tend to be successful people, and successful people tend to be competitive. There are exceptions to this, of course, but famous actors and actresses, writers and artists, and scientists and engineers don't typically get fame by being content with "also ran." They competed and, if we know their names, they won. However, there are some activities in which competitiveness is particularly highlighted. One of them is sports.

Among the celebrity examples with Mars aspecting the Nodes of the Moon, we have a wide range of famous athletes. Just to name a few, there's gymnast Simone Biles, soccer legend Pelé, mixed martial arts champion Ronda Rousey, and bicyclist Lance Armstrong with Mars conjunct the North Node. With Mars conjunct the South Node, we have basketball great Julius Erving and swimmer Mark Spitz. With the trine, we have boxer Joe Frazier and baseball hero Willie Mays. With the quincunx, there's boxer Mike Tyson and basketball's bad boy, Dennis Rodman.

As we've seen in previous chapters, the archetypical visitors brought into our lives by aspects to the Lunar Nodes can come and go. This is particularly true for professional athletes. Their careers are typically short. Sometimes, though, the Warrior leaves before the athlete is ready. For several years, Mike Tyson was the most feared boxer in the world. Then a rape conviction sent him to prison. By the time Tyson got out, the Warrior had left him, and his efforts to revive his career fizzled.

There are other kinds of competitors. There are great competitors in business, like Jack Welch, Walt Disney, and Ted Turner. However, even here we see the Warrior come and go. During the early part of his career, Walt Disney, who had Mars trine the South Node, left the business end of his enterprise to his brother. Walt felt more comfortable sticking to the creative side, developing characters and working with animators. As a result, Disney was pushed around by distributers and had one of his early characters stolen by a wily business partner. But as his business grew, Disney discovered his inner Warrior. He focused on expanding his empire, fighting the unionizing of his workers and ruthlessly crushing anyone who tried to appropriate his copyrighted characters.

Walt Disney's transition from the voice of Mickey Mouse to capitalist Warrior shows us fierceness that people with Mars aspecting the Nodes can sometimes display. This fierceness can seem quite foreign to the basic personality of that individual. Put in the context of reincarnation, we might assume that people with these aspects have come out of lives in which they were soldiers. In that case, many of them might have died in the midst of a brutal, kill-or-be-killed battle. Imagine coming into this life with that experience, that fear, and that rage still burning inside you. Wouldn't you be a little testy, particularly if someone were cutting into your business, or challenging you in the boxing ring, or fighting you for a rebound? Wouldn't you fight and compete with all your might? This is often what we see when the Warrior is aroused in the soul of a person with these aspects.

Violence

As we've already seen in examples like Ulysses S. Grant and Mike Tyson, violence sometimes plays a crucial role in the lives of people with Mars aspecting the Nodes of the Moon. The role can be quite obvious, as it was with the gangster Lucky Luciano, who had Mars trine the South Node. In other instances, the connection is less direct. Sam Peckinpah (with Mars square the Nodes) made movies that were both criticized and celebrated because of their graphic depiction of violence. Clint Eastwood (with Mars conjunct the North Node) became a household name by playing characters like the Man with No Name and Dirty Harry, who seemed to exult in violence. Stephen King (with Mars trine the South Node) writes tales of horror and mayhem. Agatha Christie (with Mars conjunct the South Node) wrote about murder. Truman Capote (also with Mars conjunct the South Node) wrote *In Cold Blood*, a book about the slaughter of a Nebraskan family and the men who committed the crime. Chuck Palahniuk (with Mars conjunct the South Node) wrote *Fight Club*.

For some people with these aspects, violence entered their lives simply because they were going too fast. Princess Diana (with Mars conjunct the North Node), 1950s bombshell Jayne Mansfield (with Mars conjunct the South Node), author Albert Camus (with Mars trine the North Node), and international playboy Aly Khan (with Mars quincunx the South Node) all died in automobile accidents.

This brings us to a tricky question: If we are to assume that aspects to the Lunar Nodes represent important karmic issues, does having Mars aspecting the Nodes indicate that you are "fated" to have violence enter your life in ways that are destructive and perhaps even deadly? This is not an issue that

modern astrologers typically like to discuss. However, given Mars's bad reputation, I think we have no choice but to deal with it directly.

The fact is that we do have a lot of people among our examples with Mars
aspecting the Nodes who did, in one way or another, become the victims of
violent events. However, in many of these cases, this outcome had as much
to do with the person's lifestyle as their horoscope. For example, the music of
rapper Tupac Shakur, who had Mars conjunct his North Node, celebrated the
"thug" lifestyle. No one knows for sure who murdered Tupac, but that lifestyle
was certainly a contributing factor. The self-destructive tendencies of Vincent
van Gogh (who had Mars square the Nodes) were evident long before he committed suicide. Likewise, the premature deaths of Janis Joplin (with Mars trine
the North Node), Jim Morrison (with Mars trine the South Node), and Amy
Winehouse (also with Mars trine the South Node) came after many years of
substance abuse.

And yet, there are also people with these aspects who have violence enter
their lives through no apparent fault of their own. Among the most notorious examples of this are Sharon Tate and Steve Parent, both of whom were
killed by the Manson "family" on August 9, 1969. Tate (who had Mars trine the
North Node) was targeted because she happened to be renting a house that
had previously been occupied by a person Charles Manson didn't like. Parent
(with Mars conjunct the North Node) had no connection to Tate or her friends.
He just had the singular misfortune of encountering the gang of murderers as
they were approaching Tate's residence. It is easy to see some element of fate
in the tragic demise of these two unwitting victims. At the same time, though,
there are victims of random acts of violence all around the world who do not
have Mars aspecting the Nodes of the Moon.

The horoscope does not give us guarantees, only potentials that we
might, or might not, fulfill. There are always factors in life that are beyond
our control, but, for most of us most of the time, the choices we make, and
not fate, dictate the course of our lives. Nothing in a horoscope should be
taken as an assurance of how or when we will die. That comes under the
heading of things we can't control, and excessively dwelling on such matters
is never going to change that.

The Archetype and You

The world needs warriors. On the battlefields and the playing fields, in business, in the arts, and in the sciences, warriors get things done. That's what you have to keep in mind if you have Mars aspecting the Nodes of the Moon, because, when this archetype comes calling, you are likely to come on stronger than you're used to, with more aggressiveness and command than is typical for you, and with a goal-driven certainty that might surprise even those who know you best. You may also step on some toes. You may say or do some things you later regret. But it's all for the purpose of finishing the job, advancing the ball, and fighting the battles that need to be fought.

The enemies and obstacles you will face will vary. The majority of you won't be called to fight in an actual war. Instead, you may just be fighting to put food on the table or to keep yourself from drowning in student debt. Some of you might be marching in the streets or making speeches for a certain cause or ideology. Or maybe you're fighting your way up the corporate ladder with an eye on a corner office with your name on the door. No matter what the fight is, however, with Mars aspecting the Nodes, it will be hard to hold back, to wait your turn, or to play it cool.

As was pointed out earlier, people with Mars aspecting the Nodes might be reincarnated from soldiers who were killed in the heat of battle. They left one life in the midst of a desperate struggle, and they come into this life primed to resume that fight. Another idea is that these people come into this life with unresolved anger issues, an inner rage that they weren't able to express because of the circumstances in which their past life lived. Establishing a factual basis for either of these ideas is unlikely. However, they do point to the importance of finding ways to properly channel the energy of Mars. Without boundaries and discipline, the fighting spirit of Mars, whatever its source, can accomplish nothing useful.

If you have Mars aspecting the Nodes of the Moon, you have to find ways to control and discipline what this archetypical visitor brings you. As always, other factors in the horoscope will be important. Some of you may also need to look outside yourself for this discipline. You might find discipline in the physical regime of sports or in the military or law enforcement. There's a reason why these Mars-related activities are stiff with rules and regulations: Martian energy, without such strictures, eventually destroys itself and everything around it.

Establishing an ethical and moral ground is important for you because the other thing this archetype will bring into your life is passion. As we have seen, this passion might be a passion for battle, for competition and winning, but it can also manifest as emotional and sexual passion. It is easy for people (mostly men, but also some women) with these aspects to get themselves entangled in messy romantic affairs. When the Mars archetype is paramount, your empathy level can suddenly drop, and you might start seeing sex partners as conquests instead of as people. That's why having the self-discipline to direct this passion in a productive and positive way is so crucial. The heart you save from breaking could very well be your own.

There are some of the difficulties having Mars aspecting the Nodes of the Moon can bring into your life. They might seem formidable, but, on the whole, they can be managed with a little self-awareness and self-discipline. Then, you have the benefits. There's a reason why there are more celebrity examples with Mars aspecting the Nodes than with the egotistic Sun or expansive Jupiter. With Mars aspecting the Nodes, you get things done. It's as simple as that. And, regardless of who you were or what you did in a past life, in this life, it's the people who get things done who get to sit at the winner's table.

CHAPTER 8

Jupiter Aspecting the North or South Nodes

We are now entering a new paradigm with regard to how aspects to the Nodes of the Moon happen. Whereas the Sun, Mercury, and Venus move through all twelve signs during a given year and Mars covers most of them, Jupiter will typically pass through only two. This slower motion means that Jupiter aspects to the Nodes last longer and that larger groups of people will share the same aspect. A conjunction by Jupiter to either of the Lunar Nodes, for example, can last as long as a month.

On the other hand, Jupiter's slower motion means that, in most cases, it makes only one or two aspects to the Nodes during a given year. This means that the total number of people in one generation born with Jupiter aspecting the Nodes is not any greater, and possibly somewhat smaller, than people born with the Sun aspecting the Nodes. This trend continues as we move through the rest of the outer planets: Saturn, Uranus, Neptune, and Pluto. The number of times when these aspects occur is reduced, but each one covers a much larger group of people.

Another difference we see with the outer planets aspecting the Nodes of the Moon is that the archetypes we associate with them tend to be more abstract and less personal. Instead of characters like the Hero or the Messenger, with the outer planets, we are dealing with concepts that are more general. For Jupiter aspecting the Nodes, that concept is faith.

Faith is the facility that allows us to face the future with hope and optimism. This might be because you have faith that there's an all-powerful deity taking care of you, or that you have a plan or an ideal that is going to make the world a better place. In either case, faith lifts us up and gives us confidence that, no matter how bad things might seem in the immediate, they will get better.

True Believers

The most common face of this archetype is the True Believer. These are people who have projected their marvelous capacity for faith onto a particular belief system. Since Jupiter has been associated with religion since ancient times, it's not surprising that these belief systems often involve faith in Jesus, Muhammad, Vishnu, or some other supernatural deity. Among the examples with Jupiter aspecting the Nodes of the Moon, we have several prominent proponents of religion. In fact, we have five True Believers who essentially started their own religions or, at least, important denominations of existing religions. With Jupiter conjunct the North Node, we have John Calvin (Calvinism) and Ellen White (Seventh-Day Adventists). With Jupiter conjunct the South Node, we have Martin Luther (Lutheranism), L. Ron Hubbard (Scientology), and Helena Blavatsky (Theosophy).

Our True Believers with Jupiter aspecting the Nodes include devout Catholics, such as poet and monk Thomas Merton and social justice activist Dorothy Day, and one bona fide Catholic saint, Sir Thomas More, who was beheaded because of his opposition to King Henry VIII's break with the Catholic Church. There are also plenty of devout Protestants, such as gospel singers Pat Boone and Tammy Faye Bakker (wife of evangelist Jim Bakker), noted evangelist Billy Graham, and the author of *Paradise Lost*, John Milton. However, it isn't just about the so-called organized religions. There are psychics like Jane Roberts (author of the Seth series) and James Van Praagh,

Zen Buddhists like Alan Watts, mystics like Carlos Castaneda, and ritual magicians like Aleister Crowley.

What seems to unite all of these True Believers with Jupiter aspecting the Nodes of the Moon is a need to see the bigger picture, a need to put their life in the context of the eternal. This is the essential function of all religions and spiritual practices. It's about taking the consciousness to a higher level, a level removed from the selfish *I* and its cavalcade of picayune problems. A level that allows for a broader, calmer, and less self-centered view of existence. Whether you do this by prayer, meditation, ritual, or magic mushrooms, the goal is always a Jupiterian expansion of awareness.

Putting these examples in the context of reincarnation, we could say that people with these aspects to the Nodes are completing a task of spiritual development begun in a past life. Maybe the person is the reincarnation of a Pagan priest or Christian mystic. Maybe they are trying to reestablish a link with the divinity that they had experienced in this past life, or maybe their spiritual development was interrupted by a sudden death. No matter how or in what state they entered their current life, according to this theory, they are in the midst of a spiritual journey that could span many lifetimes.

There are other people with Jupiter aspecting the Nodes who take their need for an expanded view of the world in a more secular direction. Friedrich Engels (who had Jupiter conjunct the North Node) had faith in the ideas of his good friend Karl Marx. This wasn't because Engels thought Marx was divine. Engels was devoted to Karl Marx's communist ideas because they explained the great social inequities of his time and offered a plan for solving them. Another guy who was captivated by these ideas was a young Russian named Vladimir Lenin, who had Jupiter trine the South Node. He took those ideas and created a revolution.

Within every belief system or political philosophy, there are people who follow along because the beliefs or ideas expressed by that system generally agree with their own. They are there mostly because it's comforting to be with people who think like they do. Then you have the True Believers, who expect much more of their belief system. They see it as a means of being transported to a higher level of thought and awareness, a level that allows them to see the social and political ills of their time in a way that might seem more objective or scientific. Sometimes it is the ideas promoted by the belief system that give them this confidence, and sometimes it's the words and insights of a leader who sees things more clearly than anyone else.

Jupiter is the planet of abundance. It fills us to the brim. That's why True Believers are so true to their belief system. The power of such complete convictions can be immensely uplifting. It gives you a kind of confidence that goes beyond your individual capacities, beyond mere ego. When applied judiciously, this power can be used to make positive changes in the real world. However, this abundance, this purity of purpose, can also be intoxicating. It can separate you from reality. It can also separate you from basic ethical and moral standards.

We see an example of this in the fact that many of the most devoted followers of Adolf Hitler during the Nazi era had Jupiter aspecting the Nodes. Faith should be a beautiful thing. It should make us better people. But so much depends on the basic character described in the horoscope. Just as the presence of a guest will expand your capacity for hope, it will also expand your fear, your anger, and your hatred. For this reason, taking on the role of the True Believer should be approached with trepidation. Faith might be ready for you, but are you ready for faith?

Faith of a Different Sort

Not everyone with Jupiter aspecting the Nodes of the Moon is a True Believer. Some find a different way of expressing this archetypical concept of faith. Instead of politics or religion, they put their faith in life itself. This type of faith features the same expansive thinking and extraordinary expectations we saw with the True Believers, but it doesn't need to be reinforced by prayer, by meditation, or by attending a rally. It is reinforced by the very process of living and all the possibilities for excitement and sensual pleasure that being alive affords us. Who needs Jesus Christ or Karl Marx when there are wine, food, sex, and laughter? Who wants to worry about the fate of their soul or the fate of society when there's a party going on?

What would be the archetypical figure for this type of faith? We could go with Greek deities like Pan or Dionysus. The free-living Shakespearian character Falstaff has, over the years, attained an almost archetypical standing. However, I've decided on a more generalized label to sum up the hedonistic, "good time," life-embracing qualities of this archetype. We will call this archetype the Libertine.

True Believers often see themselves as special. They have a special relationship with the divine or special knowledge about the state of the world. Libertine people also see themselves as special, even blessed. While other people have to restrict their pleasures out of concern for their pocketbook or dignity, these lucky children of Jupiter see no reason for such onerous constraints. Some of them might have fortunes to spend, some of them barely get by, and yet they all share a certainty that their sensuality and their devotion to having a good time will be indulged by the great and generous universe and that they will never have to suffer the consequences of their excesses. Of course, they are often disappointed, but not nearly as often as you might think.

In the context of reincarnation, we might think of these people as continuing a pattern of behavior learned in a dissolute past life. Maybe they were debauched potentates or genteel drunkards who had nothing to do but attend to their own pleasure. Or maybe the situation was just the opposite. Maybe these Libertine folks suffered hunger and deprivation in a past life. Maybe they were victims of famine, or maybe they were hermits who sacrificed their worldly possessions and worldly pleasure for the sake of their faith. Now that they're back in a living body, they've found a different concept of faith, and they are intent on making up for lost time.

Examples of people with this kind of faith include three pleasure-loving monarchs: George IV of England (with Jupiter conjunct the North Node), Charles II of England, and Louis XV of France (both with Jupiter conjunct the South Node). George's weakness for women, wine, and food made him a favorite target of the satirist of his day and ruined his health. Both Charles II and Louis XV spent more time in bed with their various mistresses than they did dealing with the affairs of state. Also with Jupiter conjunct the South Node we have Aly Khan, who was the epitome of the international playboy during the 1950s, and with Jupiter quincunx the North Node, we have Hugh Hefner, the guy who created a publication empire based on that playboy image. Also from the 1950s, we have Christine Keeler, the party girl who nearly brought down the British government, and the famous pinup model Bettie Page. Keeler had Jupiter conjunct the South Node, and Page had Jupiter trine the South Node.

Just because you put your faith in physical pleasure, that doesn't mean you can't live a productive life. Elizabeth Barrett Browning was one of the most beloved poets of the Victorian era. She was also addicted to morphine. Winston Churchill was one of the great heroes of World War II. He was also what we would now call a functioning alcoholic. In his memoir *On Writing*, Stephen King recounts his problems with alcohol and drugs, problems that reached their peak during the period when he wrote some of his most famous novels. Judy Garland's issues with substance abuse were legendary, and yet she never stopped performing.

Of course, Judy Garland is an example of how our Libertine people with Jupiter aspecting the Nodes sometimes do have to deal with consequences. She died of a drug overdose at forty-seven. Whitney Houston's problems with addiction led her to a similar fate. She had Jupiter square the Nodes. The promising careers of guitarist Brian Jones and actor River Phoenix were cut short because of drugs. Mata Hari's scandalous lifestyle had as much to do with her dying in front of a firing squad as any amount of spying. The lifestyle of Jeffrey Epstein, who had Jupiter square the Nodes, led to his downfall.

It is not uncommon for these Libertine people with Jupiter aspecting the Nodes of the Moon to change their concept of faith and jump to the True Believer category. After her modeling career was over, Bettie Page began studying to become a Christian missionary. Pop singer Belinda Carlisle struggled with addiction during her early career with the Go-Go's. She credits her conversion to Buddhism with helping her get sober. In his youth, George W. Bush was known as a free-living party boy. After a religious conversion, he put this lifestyle aside and entered politics.

For other Libertine folks, the price for their good fortune is paid by someone else. The Impressionist painter Pierre-Auguste Renoir, a Pisces with Jupiter trine his South Node, never had a fixed address until he was well over forty. There was always a friend who was willing to let the easygoing Renoir crash for a while, set up his easel, and knock out a few masterpieces. And there was always a plump working-class girl willing to pose for the painter and join him in bed. However, when one of these women became pregnant, Renoir seemed to be in a pickle. He was in no position to support a wife and child. So the infant was sent away to an orphanage. No one knows for sure what happened to this child, but most newborns sent to these institutions during this period in France died during their first year.

As always, how you deal with Jupiter aspecting the Nodes depends greatly on what else is going on in your horoscope. When these aspects occur in charts that already show a proclivity toward addiction, they can be troublesome. Tendencies in the chart toward violence or extremism can also be expanded. On the other hand, some people with these aspects seem to get off easy, though the same might not apply to their friends and family.

Exceptions

The long list of examples of people with Jupiter aspecting the Nodes of the Moon contains many people from both the True Believer category and the Libertine group. However, there are also a lot of people who do not fit neatly into either category. They seem to be the exceptions. With aspects to the Nodes of the Moon, we have to expect exceptions. The archetype has to have a horoscope congenial to its aims in order to fully exert its influence.

Of course, there are also different degrees of being a True Believer or a Libertine. Many people have periods during their youth or maybe during a midlife crisis when they might take on the Libertine role. Likewise, some people go through periods when they are religious or intensely involved in a political or social cause. These detours might be regarded as merely phases, but they could also be evidence of this archetypical visitor making a call.

It may be that some of our exceptions are people who have had, or will have in the future, one of these Jupiter phases. They may also be people who are or were quiet about their beliefs and philosophies. Included among them are many celebrities who espouse worthy causes. For some of them, we might assume that this is just about getting some good press. However, there may be others for whom these causes are actually quite meaningful. However, we also have to keep in mind that faith is a delicate commodity. Perhaps more than any other archetype, this one requires just the right balance of intellect and emotion, rationality and imagination. It only takes a small amount of doubt to create an atmosphere in which real devotion and trust (religious, secular, or hedonistic) cannot grow. This is what makes faith so precious and, compared to some of our other archetypes, so rare.

The Archetype and You

If you have Jupiter aspecting the Nodes of the Moon in your horoscope, you have been given something very special. That is the gift of faith. You stand at the top of the mountain. You see the world in all its breadth and beauty. And you see the ways that it can be better. Arriving at such an exalted point of view can be exhilarating. It could be a peak experience that makes everything else that has happened in your life seem trivial and insufficient. It makes no difference if you are putting your faith in a divine being, a secular cause, or your inevitable good fortune; you feel special, you feel a power greater than yourself surging through your being. You feel a confidence in the correctness of your actions that might seem scary. And it should be, because that confidence, when it is misplaced, can get you into a whole lot of trouble.

We've seen several examples of this kind of trouble. It can come out of people putting their faith in the wrong cause or leader. It can also come out of people surrendering their objectivity to a religion, a political theory, or their ability to survive risky behavior. The antidote for these troubles, at least for the True Believers, is making sure that your belief system is based on hope and not fear, and that its objective is making things better for everyone, not just for you or the people who look like you.

With Jupiter aspecting the Nodes, you are not likely to be satisfied with the belief system that was handed to you by your parents or tradition. You need to branch out, or at least take those beliefs to a higher level. Celebrating your faith and exploring all its possibilities is part of the journey. However, you also have to be willing to accept the limitations of your belief system.

You need to understand what it can bring you and what it can't. Being aware of these limitations need not be a source of doubt. Nor should this awareness be seen as evidence of heresy or bad faith. You are simply making sure that you have some say in where your faith takes you.

With this archetype, your real enemy is not heresy or doubt. It is excess. You might think that the danger of excess applies only to the Libertine people. After all, they're the ones with the hangovers and the lower back tattoos. However, there is more than one way to become intoxicated. People who are intoxicated with the love of a superior being or belief system may seem quite benign, but history shows us something different. History is filled with great atrocities committed by True Believers who thought they were answering the call of a higher power or a worthy doctrine to make the world a better place.

Definitely, this is an archetype that must be handled with extreme care, but that's because of the power that it can convey. It is not a power that is limited to the individual, as we saw with the Hero or the Divine Feminine. It is a power that can be shared with dozens, hundreds, even millions of people. For the True Believer, this power can give you the opportunity to make history. For the Libertine, it can give you a chance to share in the great joy of living. This is the true gift of faith. It is a gift that goes beyond certainty in the correctness of your cause or the rewards of some imagined paradise. It is the gift of feeling yourself part of a gleefully blessed and ever-expanding universe.

And what about the exceptions, the people who have Jupiter aspecting the Nodes of the Moon but seem unable to access or accept this gift of faith? If you are one of these exceptions, you need not give up hope. Faith is delicate and capricious, but it can be cultivated. It can be helped along. You just have to create a space in your life in which it can grow. This may mean pruning back your practicality, your pride, and your cynicism. It may mean finding reasons for hope in a world that so often feels hopeless. But, if you can do this and you have the patience and persistence to make that little garden grow, it can become a place that brings light and joy to every corner of your life.

CHAPTER 9

Saturn Aspecting the North or South Nodes

With Jupiter, we saw the liberating power of faith, both in the form of the True Believer and the Libertine. What we get with Saturn aspecting the Nodes of the Moon is, in many ways, completely the opposite. The function of Saturn is to draw boundaries, confine, define, and provide structure. Saturn replies to Jupiter's optimism with cold, hard facts. Saturn responds to Jupiter's liberation by setting limits and building walls. Saturn answers Jupiter's faith with doubt.

Doubt

Doubt is an essential human function. None of us would survive very long on Earth without it. Doubt is what causes us to double-check our facts, measure twice, and look before we leap. There are times when doubt limits us, when it denies us the thrill of blasting off into the unknown. However, there are also times when mistrusting the untried, the unproven, and the unlikely can save us a whole lot of grief. Doubt keeps us alert and watchful. Doubt also shows us our limitations and the pitfalls of too much confidence and too much self-indulgence. Faith without doubt is unstructured and unreliable. It is a doorway without a door, a window without a pane.

The concept of doubt that comes to us with Saturn aspecting the Nodes of the Moon, however, is of a more fundamental sort. It is a doubt that is rooted in the alignment, or misalignment, of our wills, our desires, and our aspirations with those of the world around us. It is doubt about our place in the society in which we live and the efficacy of the work we do. This doubt and pessimism are often so automatic, so engrained, that we might not even be aware of the degree to which they color our perspective on life or shadow our self-esteem. Doubt, in some cases, causes us to conclude that life or the world or even the universe is against us, that we never had a chance, that we are misfits, outsiders, and losers.

Some people with Saturn aspecting the Lunar Nodes feel this fundamental doubt and give up. "Why should I even try," they say. However, other people take these misgivings as a challenge. Doubt calls upon them to put aside the trite, the insubstantial, and the unrealistic and focus on what is necessary and important. Doubt dispels their delusions and their impossible dreams and helps them become more effective people.

How a person with these aspects reacts to this archetypical doubt depends greatly on what else is going on in their horoscope. Some people are more inclined to give in while others are hardwired to take the challenge. Nonetheless, there is always an element of choice. With Saturn, fate is almost always an extension of character. Good choices and sound decisions may not eliminate the deep sense of self-doubt that often comes with these aspects, but they can make your road through the darkness much easier.

In looking for an archetypical figure to represent this doubt, we could call up the Cynic, the Disbeliever, or the Skeptic. However, I think a fairer description of Saturn as an archetype is the Teacher. This is a Teacher who is firm and strict, a Teacher who is constantly testing the effectiveness of our ideas and the strength of our character. This is a tough, merciless Teacher who will look down at us with seemingly endless disapproval until that blessed day when we prove ourselves worthy.

Surrender

In September 1957, *On the Road* was published, and its author, Jack Kerouac, became an overnight success. This might seem like every writer's dream come true, but for Kerouac, it became a nightmare and a test for which he was ill prepared. As America's newest literary star, Kerouac was expected to submit to interviews in print and on radio. He was also expected to be the voice of the "Beat" generation, to be the "King of the Beats."

Kerouac not only had Saturn conjunct the North Node of the Moon in his natal chart, but the publication of *On the Road* coincided with an important transit of Saturn in his natal horoscope. The Teacher that had been with him his whole life, pressuring him to perform and to type, type, type until he not only finished *On the Road* but several other books, was now demanding Kerouac prove himself in another way. Not as a writer. That was too easy. He was called upon to prove himself as an intellectual, or maybe as an anti-intellectual, and as the spokesman for a new generation. The Teacher had laid this test on Kerouac's desk. He looked it over, threw down his pencil, and ran off looking for the nearest bar.

Alcohol had been a big part of Jack Kerouac's life long before 1957, but the events of that year sent him on a bender that essentially did not end until his death twelve years later. Kerouac felt the weight of Saturn aspecting the Nodes of the Moon and gave in to it. Though he continued to write and publish, Kerouac spent most of his remaining years living in seclusion with his mother.

Some people with these aspects try to hide from this Teacher by aligning themselves with stronger, more confident people. Despite her phenomenal popularity (she also had the Moon aspecting the Nodes), Marilyn Monroe was burdened with Saturn trine her Lunar Node. Throughout her life, Monroe sought to bury her doubt in relationships with dominant men. A generation earlier, the silent screen siren, Clara Bow, tried the same thing. In both cases, doubt won.

Answering your doubt by handing your choices off to someone else might seem like a way of escaping the deep misgivings about your self-worth that Saturn aspecting the Nodes of the Moon can engender, but it rarely ends well.

It's your choices that the Teacher is watching, and letting another person choose for you is almost always the wrong choice.

It is all too easy to find sad examples of this phenomenon. Three of the women who were part of the Manson family had Saturn aspecting the Nodes: Squeaky Fromme, with Saturn trine the North Node; Susan Atkins, with Saturn square the Nodes; and Patricia Krenwinkel, also with Saturn square the Nodes. (Krenwinkel had both the Moon and Saturn aspecting the Nodes.) Similarly, Myra Hindley, who had Saturn square the Nodes, surrendered her choices to a psychopath named Ian Brady and went to jail as an accomplice to the brutal murders committed by that man.

As these examples illustrate, surrendering to the self-doubt imposed upon us by this archetype can have horrendous results. Surrender doesn't free you from doubt. It only makes you likely to become its prisoner. The human beings onto whom you project the archetype of the Saturnian Teacher might seem easier to please. After all, all they usually require is that you perform certain real-world tasks, like cooking dinner or helping them commit a crime. But the doubt that comes with Saturn aspecting the Nodes is rooted in your soul. It will not be silenced by the praise you earn from other people. It has to be faced, and the only one who can face it is you.

Angry Doubt

The Teacher can make you angry. Always doubting you, always asking you questions to which you don't have an answer, always judging your choices, telling you to obey the rules, limiting your desires, and keeping you in your own damn lane. Among our examples of people with Saturn aspecting the Nodes of the Moon, we have several people who let this anger get the best of them. Instead of facing their self-doubt, they lash out at the world around them. These examples include Oklahoma City bomber Timothy McVeigh (with Saturn conjunct the North Node), assassin James Earl Ray (also with Saturn conjunct the South Node), Columbine High School killer Eric Harris (with Saturn trine the South Node), Lee Harvey Oswald (with Saturn conjunct the South Node), and the man who killed Oswald, Jack Ruby (with Saturn on the North Node).

Some people with these aspects have good reason to dread and despise the Teacher. Life has given them disadvantages that make it easy for self-doubt to grow. These disadvantages might have to do with poverty or a person's upbringing. They might have to do with class, race, gender, and other issues over which the person has no control. We can understand the anger that these people might feel. At the same time, though, there are other people with Saturn aspecting the Nodes of the Moon who seem to have all the advantages that a person could hope for and yet still lash out against their doubt.

Nathan Leopold and Richard Loeb were both teenagers from wealthy families living in an affluent section of Chicago during the 1920s. They were both highly intelligent young men with a great future ahead of them. Then, in 1924, these two youngsters decided that they were so smart that they could pull off the perfect crime. They kidnapped and murdered a younger boy and used an elaborate scheme to confuse law enforcement and conceal their involvement in the crime. Needless to say, their plan fell apart, and both young men were sentenced to life in prison.

The crime of Loeb and Leopold has been called a "thrill" killing, but the violence of their actions points to something more than momentary excitement. It points to a deep-seated reservoir of anger. What could have inspired such anger in two young men who seemed to have everything going for them? Both horoscopes contain strong aspects to Mars and other explosive indicators, but what really unites the two charts are aspects by Saturn to the Nodes of the Moon. Loeb had Saturn conjunct the South Node. Leopold had Saturn quincunx the North Node. Along with their privilege and intelligence, they shared this hidden influencer and the doubt that it brought into their lives. The crime that these two young men committed, which at the time was considered the "crime of the century," was their ill-conceived response to that doubt.

Fighting Through the Doubt

What makes the choice made by Leopold and Loeb so egregious is the fact that we have many examples of people who felt the doubt of Saturn aspecting the Nodes and accepted its challenge. These are people who succeeded and did remarkable things despite the ominous shadow cast by this archetype. Within this group, we have tennis champions Arthur Ashe, Monica Seles, and Martina Navratilova. We have supermodel Tyra Banks, magazine publisher Helen Gurley Brown, author Louisa May Alcott, artist Rosa Bonheur, activist Malcolm X, and politicians Franklin Roosevelt and Hillary Clinton.

All these people had good reason to doubt themselves and feel that they were swimming against the current of their times. For Malcolm, Ashe, and Banks, it was a matter of race. For Helen Gurley Brown, Louisa May Alcott, Rosa Bonheur, and Hillary Clinton, it was their gender. For Navratilova, it was her sexual orientation. For Monica Seles, it was a random act of violence perpetrated by a crazed fan. For Franklin Roosevelt, it was polio.

To better understand how doubt can hijack a person's life and the importance of making the right choices, we need to compare the lives of two professional golfers, both of whom had Saturn conjunct their South Node. The first is Jack Nicklaus, a name that is probably familiar even to people who know nothing about golf. The other is George Archer, who was a contemporary of Nicklaus and, like him, the winner of several major tournaments, including the prestigious Masters. However, if you've never heard of him, don't feel bad. That's exactly the way George Archer wanted it.

Archer suffered from a learning disability that left him functionally illiterate. So, while Nicklaus was always available for interviews and appeared in ads endorsing a wide variety of products, Archer avoided the press and turned down lucrative endorsement deals because he feared that these activities would reveal his inability to read. By insisting on keeping his illiteracy a secret (it was only revealed after his death by his wife), George Archer gave in to his doubt. Like Jack Kerouac, the test had been laid before him, and he decided to walk away.

Jack Nicklaus, in the meantime, became one of the most recognizable names in sports. However, Nicklaus was not without doubts of his own. In a 2015 interview, Nicklaus admitted that his faith in himself never quite matched his public image. He called himself an underachiever. Apparently, Nicklaus also felt the presence of this doubting guest in his life. He just refused to give in to it.

Losers

Of course, not giving in to your doubts is easy when you're winning. It's much more of a challenge when you are not, when you find yourself paddling against the stream of public opinion with the whole world watching. This next group of examples are people who did just that. Some people might call them losers, but they represent the kind of losers the world desperately needs.

In this group, we have Ralph Nader (with Saturn conjunct the North Node), who has spent his life fighting (he also has Mars aspecting the Nodes) against the power of big corporations and big money in American politics. We also have Al Gore (with Saturn square the Nodes), who has led the way in warning people about climate change, and Yitzhak Rabin (with Saturn conjunct the North Node), who struggled to bring peace between Israel and the Palestinians. And then there's Dr. Patch Adams (also with Saturn conjunct the North Node), who has long been an advocate of bringing down the cost of medical care in this country.

Another example of this type of loser is George McGovern, who had Saturn conjunct the North Node of the Moon. In 1972, McGovern ran for president with a promise to end the Vietnam War. He was defeated by Richard Nixon in a landslide of historic proportions. However, when we consider how the Vietnam War eventually ended and the long, disgraceful shadow that it has cast over the politics and consciousness of this nation, it would seem that George McGovern came closer to being right about this issue than any of the "winners."

In 1936, a German boxer named Max Schmeling (with Saturn conjunct the South Node) was challenging a Black American fighter named Joe Louis for the heavyweight title of the world. Despite Schmeling's abhorrence of the idea, Joseph Goebbels's Nazi propaganda machine continually billed him as a representative of the "master race." This turned Schmeling's match with Louis into a major event fraught with political and racial implications. Louis defeated Schmeling in the first round and, even though Schmeling was a skilled boxer and had previously been a world champion, it is that loss for which he is most remembered.

It is sometimes possible to turn the things that make you appear to be a loser into assets. Actress Carrie Fisher, who had Saturn conjunct the North Node, wrote books and did one-woman shows describing her struggles with substance abuse and mental illness. Emily Dickinson (also with Saturn conjunct the North Node) didn't seem to mind being seen as the eccentric "old maid" of Amherst. It kept people at a distance and gave her more time to write poetry. When the British singer George Michael (with Saturn quincunx the North Node) was outed as a gay man in 1998, his career as a male sex symbol may have ended, but his career as a performer continued on a sounder and more honest basis.

As these examples illustrate, being a loser is not always a bad thing. However, in order to make losing a positive force, you have to embrace the reasons for that loss. You have to embrace your deficiency, your bad luck, and your doubt. You have to understand that the odds are stacked up against you and accept that as a challenge. Things might not go well for you. It might seem that you are taking a pounding like the one Joe Louis gave Max Schmeling, but if you believe in what you're doing and understand that today's losses can build tomorrow's victories, you have nothing to fear.

The Archetype and You

For some of you, the self-doubt that Saturn aspecting the Nodes brings into your life will show itself in obvious and conventional ways. It may come out of health concerns or physical infirmities. Or it could be things like poverty, a lack of education, or traumas stemming from your childhood that make you feel like a loser or an outsider. You might think that you deserve a break. However, with this archetype, there are no exemptions. Regardless of how unfairly life may have treated you, you still have to face your doubt. You still have to answer to the Teacher.

In other instances, it is our own bad decisions that bring doubt into our lives. With Jupiter aspecting the Nodes, people often think (sometimes correctly) that they can escape the consequences of their actions. With Saturn, that is not an option. There is no playing truant from this Teacher. Regardless of the worldly buffers—like wealth, position, and popularity—that you might think are installed in your life, the consequences of your actions will seek you out.

All of this makes Saturn's aspects to the Nodes of the Moon sound like the furies of Greek mythology, who sought out and punished those who had offended the gods. It is easy to arrive at the assumption that people with these aspects come into this life with extraordinary karmic debts and that the doubt that haunts them stems from misdeeds committed in a past life. Of course, if you are the person born with one of these aspects in your chart, you might consider this assumption a bit heavy-handed. I tend to agree. We can assume that these aspects indicate that you are being tested. That's what Saturn the Teacher is all about. But we can't really know the cosmic circumstances behind those tests. Maybe it is a matter of bad behavior in a past life, or maybe it's the universe's way of getting you into better shape, spiritually speaking, for what's waiting for you in the next life.

So how do you pass the tests given to us by this stern and distant Teacher? The only way is to face your doubt: touch it, caress it, and experience it fully. You have to avoid pitfalls like surrender, self-pity, and anger. You have to accept the idea that you might be called a "loser" by some people. You have to understand all of this, and then you have to keep on doing your best.

This is the test that this guest brings us. It's not about how smart or talented you are. It's about feeling the full weight of human limitation, human culpability, and human error and continuing with your human affairs. This is not to say that you don't learn anything from these tests. You will learn that there is no shame in failure and that defeat is often the first step toward victory. You will learn that winning matters less than being on the right side, and that the right side is always the side that feeds your soul. What Saturn teaches us is that being human is not easy. There are a lot of ways that you can mess it up. That's what the doubt is for. To keep you on the right track.

CHAPTER 10

Uranus Aspecting the North or South Nodes

We now enter the realm of the outer planets, the planets that are not visible to the naked eye and were unknown to ancient astrologers. Here, everything seems to slow down and become more general. During a period of twelve months, Uranus will move somewhere between 6 and 9 degrees. The Nodes move backward along the ecliptic at a steady clip of 18 degrees a year. That means that the movement of Uranus during a year will be, at most, only half the distance covered by the Nodes. Conjunctions between Uranus and the Nodes can last anywhere from four to eight months. On the other hand, there are years in which Uranus makes no aspect to the Nodes at all. This gives the aspects of Uranus and the other outer planets to the Nodes an almost generational flavor.

It might seem that this would make the influence of Uranus aspecting the Nodes difficult to discern. After all, if most of the people you grew up with share this aspect, it would follow that you all would share similar attitudes and behaviors and that those attitudes and behaviors would seem normal to you. This is where the concept of the planet aspecting the Nodes as an outlier or unseen influencer comes into play. The influence of Uranus aspecting the Nodes of the Moon can come to us at different times in our lives, and each of us will react to it in a different way according to what's happening in our natal horoscopes. You might have been dealing with Uranus aspecting the Nodes while you were still in grade school, while other people you know might not feel that influence until they are in college. And each of you will deal with these aspects in a different way depending on the placement of the more personal planets in your horoscope.

Mischief

Uranus is considered the planet of revolution, disruption, and sudden change. It is the planet that pushes us to defy the status quo and look for a better way. It might seem then that each of these periodic Uranus aspects to the Lunar Nodes would give us a generation of little Che Guevaras, but there are many different kinds of revolutions, and the vast majority of them don't involve politics. They are personal, having to do with your reaction to the circumstances you face every day. This could mean fighting with your parents, or against the conventional morality of your community, or with the strictures of your profession or social status. It could also mean breaking the rules just for the hell of it and finding small, personal ways to jam the gears of that great machine we call the status quo. In other words, creating mischief.

We tend to think of mischief as a bad thing and of mischief-makers as undesirable. Though it is true that we have plenty of examples when this is the case and that the urge to create mischief brings about negative results, there are also times when a little mischief is exactly what we need, when it reveals to us that there is life beyond the crushing sameness of conformity. This is true of all of us, but it has particular relevance to people with Uranus aspecting the Nodes. Their job is to show the rest of us that the rules can be broken and that the unexpected can happen. The results might not always be pleasant, and sometimes they can be downright tragic, but, when it's done right and at the right time, that little bit of mischief can be both refreshing and, on a deeper level, liberating.

The Contrarian

Sometimes the best way to create mischief is to simply do the unexpected, to zig left when everyone expects you to zag right, to say no when the reasonable option would be to say yes. People with Uranus aspecting the Nodes of the Moon seem to take pleasure in being contrary and overturning the assumptions of other people, particularly figures of authority. They love the look on our faces when they do something that, at first glance, seems to make no sense. However, very often, a closer look reveals that this person is aiming toward higher truth, one that can open our minds and free us from our prejudices.

In 1947, an Oscar-winning screenwriter named Ring Lardner Jr. was brought before the House Committee on Un-American Activity and asked to reveal the names of people in the film industry who had belonged to the Communist Party. He said no. This was not what people expected him to do. Saying no to these congressmen meant a prison sentence for contempt. More importantly, Lardner was placing his career as a screenwriter in serious jeopardy. By refusing to cooperate, he risked being blacklisted by the movie-making industry. But Ring Lardner Jr. was a brave man. He was willing to take those risks, which turned out to be all too real, in order to stand up for his principles. Moreover, Lardner also had Uranus conjunct his North Node, so we might say that taking the contrary position was something he was fated to do.

We see this same contrarian spirit in the work of feminists like Simone de Beauvoir (with Uranus conjunct the South Node) and Betty Friedan (with Uranus trine the North Node). We also see it in Cesar Chavez's (Uranus square the Nodes) efforts to unionize farmworkers, Michael Moore's (Uranus conjunct the South Node) movies, Ronan Farrow's (Uranus square the Nodes) journalism, and even in Evel Knievel's (Uranus conjunct the South Node) daredevil stunts. Uranus aspecting the Nodes didn't provide the courage and dedication that these people displayed, but it did provide a desire to shake up the status quo and tweak the noses of all the doubters and figures of authority who said it couldn't or shouldn't be done.

The Contrarians with Uranus aspecting the Nodes of the Moon often appear to be rebelling against the norms of their society, so it should come as no surprise that James Dean, the star of the generation-defining movie *Rebel*

Without a Cause, had Uranus conjunct his North Node. Likewise, Jack Kerouac, author of *On the Road*, had Uranus quincunx the North Node. Hunter S. Thompson was another writer who proudly displayed this rebellious contrarian spirit. Thompson, who also had Uranus quincunx the North Node, rode with the Hell's Angels and lampooned the 1968 Republican Convention all in the name of his first-person, dope-addled style of journalism. We see the rebellious Contrarian at work in the music and lifestyles of rockers Jim Morrison and Marilyn Manson. In another era and in a different way, Wolfgang Amadeus Mozart was a Uranian rebel. Comedians John Belushi, Margaret Cho, Cheech Marin, and Roseanne Barr made being a contrarian part of their acts.

This is not to say that being a Contrarian always has positive results. There are times when it brings out hatred and prejudice instead of courage and creativity. During the French Revolution, Maximilien Robespierre (with Uranus trine the North Node) was a leader of the most radical of the revolutionaries. He was determined to say no to the privileges and abuses of the class that had ruled France for centuries. However, Robespierre's merciless determination resulted in the slaughter of many innocent people. The Marquis de Sade, who had Uranus conjunct the South Node, expressed his contrarian ideas with his pen, writing lurid stories that featured extreme sex play and sacrilege against the Catholic Church.

Choosing the route of the Contrarian will almost always get you noticed. It can also be the source of much mischievous amusement. However, the Uranian archetype is a treacherous playmate. It will test your character and stretch your moral standards. This is particularly the case when factors in your natal horoscope make you more susceptible to the rebellious influence of this archetype. Knowing when to stop is the key, and for some people with these aspects, that stopping point is difficult to find. It took a prison sentence to stop Sade and the guillotine to stop Robespierre.

The Trickster

For some people with Uranus aspecting the Nodes, being a Contrarian is too obvious. They prefer the role of the Trickster. The Trickster doesn't directly oppose the status quo. Instead, it subverts it through actions and statements that slip between the cracks of the imposing edifice of convention to reveal its weaknesses. Many of the Contrarians I've named were also Tricksters. One often leads to the other. Still, the mischief of the Trickster tends to be more playful. The goal of this archetype is not to see the system collapse; it's to have a bit of fun at the system's expense.

Andy Warhol, who had Uranus trine the South Node, turned the Trickster's antics into art. He didn't invent the style called Pop Art, but he was among the first to fully exploit its subversive potential. Likewise, Bob Dylan, who had Uranus trine the North Node, didn't invent folk music. He just gave it an extra edge. There had been plenty of controversial DJs on the radio before Howard Stern arrived, but Stern's Trickster instincts, combined with a substantial ego (he had Uranus on his South Node and the Sun on his North Node), took that job description to a higher level.

However, most people with Uranus aspecting the Nodes of the Moon don't make being the Trickster a full-time job. Instead, the Trickster pops up in their lives at odd moments, skewing their behavior in strange and quietly rebellious ways. In his working life, Charles Dodgson, who had Uranus conjunct the South Node, was a staid professor of mathematics, but when he was with children, he became Lewis Carroll, the inventor of fantastic tales and adventures. Greta Garbo, with Uranus trine the North Node, retired from acting at the peak of her career because she decided that she'd rather be alone. Led Zeppelin guitarist Jimmy Page, with Uranus trine the South Node, lived in the mansion that had formally been the seat of the famous mage Aleister Crowley.

There are other people with these aspects, like President Bill Clinton and televangelist Jimmy Swaggart, for whom the mischief created by the Trickster results in scandal and embarrassment. The Trickster likes doing things on the sly. It likes breaking the rules and getting away with it. The person with Uranus aspecting the Nodes might seem quite upstanding and conventional, but this only increases the Trickster's delight. Likewise, being found out, as these hidden Tricksters almost always are, is by no means a problem. While the perpetrators might seem to suffer greatly in terms of their position and reputation and show genuine contrition, the Trickster within them remains unmoved. To the Trickster, it's just part of the joke.

The Generational Factor

In 1900, Uranus was conjunct the North Node of the Moon for most of that year. German males born in that year would have been too young to fight in World War I, but they would have come of age during the tumultuous period just after the war, when Germany was suffering intense privation and political instability. Many people born in Germany during the conjunction of Uranus to the North Node became involved in the divisive politics of the time. They weren't content with just making mischief. They wanted a revolution. Some became ardent communists, while others were lured by the hateful rhetoric of Adolf Hitler. Not surprisingly, three of them rose to prominence in the Nazi Party: Heinrich Himmler, the head of the SS; Hans Frank, the Nazi boss in Poland and the man who oversaw the Holocaust there; and Martin Bormann, Hitler's secretary.

However, not every German born in 1900 with Uranus conjunct the North Node was ready to sign on to Hitler's revolution. Composer Kurt Weill (who wrote the music for *The Threepenny Opera*) fled Germany and came to the United States. Likewise, psychologist Erich Fromm found sanctuary in the United States after Hitler took power. Wolfgang Pauli, a physicist who was already well known in the scientific world by the 1930s, retreated to Switzerland, where he partnered with Carl Jung in the study of synchronicity. For these men, it was the disruptive qualities of Uranus that dominated. They were forced to make drastic changes in the course of their lives because of factors beyond their control.

In 1915, Uranus came around to conjunct the North Node again. In this year, the actress Ingrid Bergman was born, as well as singers Edith Piaf and Frank Sinatra. The mischief created by these three people seems to have mostly involved their love lives. The conjunction of Uranus and the North Node in the summer of 1946 has proven to be a momentous one for the United States. Three future US presidents were born during this period: in June, Donald Trump; in July, George W. Bush; and in August, Bill Clinton.

As stated earlier, even though Uranus aspects to the Nodes can last a long time and impact a lot of people born during the same month or even year, the way in which each of those people deals with this archetype can vary widely depending on their circumstances and personalities.

The Lightning Strike

The Contrarian and the Trickster get to impose their mischief onto the world, but this is not the case for everyone with Uranus aspecting the Nodes. For many, mischief is imposed on them by events beyond their control, like the political climate into which they were born. They become less the perpetrators of mischief and more its victim. The standards and conventions that are shattered might force them to flee their homeland or make other drastic changes in the way they live their lives. Often, in keeping with the archetypes' character, these changes are sudden and unexpected. They come into our lives like a bolt of lightning and play havoc with our plans and expectations.

These lightning strikes don't have to be "bad" or destructive. We can see this in the three presidents I named. Not only are they from the same baby boomer generation, but they are also united by how unexpected their rise to the highest office in the land was. Clinton was a draft-dodging, small-town boy with a history of sex scandals. Bush was the ne'er-do-well son of a previous president. It was his straight-arrow brother who was supposed to get the job. Add to this the improbable election of Donald Trump in 2016, and you get an idea of how having Uranus aspecting the Nodes can bring the bizarrely unexpected into a person's life.

But let's not stop there. We have two more unlikely US presidents with Uranus conjunct the North Node: Abraham Lincoln and Barack Obama. Lincoln was a country lawyer who only won the nomination of his party because the much more famous front-runners canceled each other out. Lincoln became a hero to Black Americans, but even he probably would not have been able to envision a day when a Black man with an African name would occupy the Oval Office.

For others, though, the injection of the Uranian archetypes has ominous results. When King Louis XVI of France (who had Uranus quincunx the North Node of the Moon) married Marie Antoinette of Austria (who had Uranus conjunct the South Node), neither expected their life together would end at the guillotine. The Confederate general Stonewall Jackson (who had Uranus conjunct the South Node) didn't expect that, while returning to camp from a victorious battle, he would be shot by his own men. Likewise, Patty Hearst (also with Uranus conjunct the South Node) didn't expect to be kidnapped by a rogue band of left-wing terrorists. Sometimes the mischief played on us by Uranus can seem cruel and malicious.

The Archetype and You

It's obvious from the examples we've seen that having Uranus aspecting the Nodes can be a lot to deal with. This archetype can push you into the role of the Contrarian and put you at odds with the society in which you live. It can chase you from your home, destroy your career, and shred your reputation. It can also make you famous and significantly raise your status in life. The problem is that it's hard to predict which direction this hidden influencer is taking you. A thrilling climb is sometimes followed by a precipitous drop. A defiant act that earns you recrimination at one point in your life could later make you a hero. Obviously, other factors in your horoscope will play a part in this, as will the choices you make and the behaviors in which you engage. But even when all these things are considered, having Uranus aspecting the Lunar Nodes in your horoscope is likely to make you nervous.

Not everyone with these aspects gets the full brunt of the Uranian archetype. Horoscopes that accent stability and patience can dampen the mischievous influence of this archetype. They can also help you deal with the disruptions that Uranus can sometimes bring into your life. However, even when the influence of these aspects is muted, it is still likely that you will sometimes have difficulty dealing with figures of authority. You will also have a low tolerance for people who are taking themselves or what they do too seriously. You might find it very hard to walk away from such people without saying or doing something that throws them off balance or punctures their self-importance.

Also, as we've seen, the Trickster has a way of inserting itself into your life at random moments. Maybe you think you have this archetype under control. Maybe you see yourself as a calm, disciplined person immune to the allure of mischief. Then you say or do something outrageous, something that has all the people who know you scratching their heads. "Where did that come from?" they're thinking. It came from the great mystery to which we are linked by aspects to the Nodes. It came from the archetype of Uranus and the Trickster. Don't waste your time trying to explain it, even to yourself. The Trickster was just having a laugh.

Of course, the chaos this archetype can bring into our lives is not always a laughing matter. Sometimes Uranus can put you in the crosshairs of major political and social upheaval. In these instances, it is easy to assume that people who suffer because of the mischief brought into their lives by Uranus aspecting the Nodes are paying for some crime or misdeed committed in a past life. However, I'm not so sure that the universe works in this simple tit-for-tat manner. The game being played here is much longer than one, two, or even a few dozen lives, and the rules are likely much more complex than we could ever know.

Personally, I don't think that life is ever a punishment. Rather, it is an experiment. If you have Uranus aspecting the Nodes, particularly if the rest of your chart supports its disruptive tendencies, that experiment will likely be more radical than most. The influence of this archetype can take you to some places you never expected to be and get you into situations for which you are ill prepared. Don't be surprised by this and, most of all, don't panic. Your experiment is just playing itself out. The result might not be what you anticipated, but if you knew for sure what the result would be, it wouldn't be an experiment.

At the same time, though, you can't afford to be a passive passenger on the big bus of history. You have to stay alert, mindful that sudden disruptions in the political or social environment could have special significance for you. Maybe you'll be lucky. Maybe you won't have to live through what the Chinese called "interesting times." But even in uninteresting times, people with these aspects have to pay close attention to what's going on in the world around them and remember that, regardless of our preparations, the Trickster will always find a way to surprise us.

CHAPTER 11

Neptune Aspecting the
North or South Nodes

While Uranus can cover as much as 9 degrees in a twelve-month period, Neptune will typically move no more than 3. This means that any aspect between Neptune to the Nodes of the Moon can last for months, giving them a generational quality similar to what we saw with Uranus. As with the Uranus aspects, what makes the way each person within that generation manifests this aspect unique is the way in which the archetype interacts with the rest of that individual's horoscope. However, with Neptune, there is an additional factor at play. Neptune is, by its very nature, amorphous. The symbolism of Neptune covers everything from the most profound spiritual experience to the tackiest pop culture craze. The saintly mystic peacefully meditating on the divine is a creature of Neptune. So is the latest viral cat video. Neptune represents our irrational response to a world that, most of the time, seems all too rational and real. For some of us, that response is to reach toward a higher state of consciousness. For others, it is aimless escapism.

Vision

In order to understand how Neptune functions when it aspects the Nodes of the Moon, you have to leave behind the realm of rational thought. Many people (and most Capricorns) have a plan for where they'll be in five, ten, or twenty years. People with Neptune aspecting the Nodes have a vision. What's the difference? With a plan, you are tied to reality. With a vision, you are not. A plan consists of a number of steps that get you to a desired goal. A vision transports you from where you are now to your goal without concern for what happens in between. In terms of practicality, a plan is always preferable to a vision. But no plan, no matter how successfully it is completed, can give you the pure exhilaration of a vision realized.

There are many different types of visions. Great artists and great scientists have to be, at some level, visionaries. They are not just recording the truth about the real world. They are recording their vision of that truth, and it is that visionary quality that raises their work to a higher level. Obviously, vision plays a big role in the lives of people who are spiritually oriented. Some of them actually have "visions." However, vision is just as important to the businessperson, the tradesperson, and the small business owner. The bank is going to want to see your business plan, but what gets you up early every morning and keeps you working into the night is your vision of what your business could be.

If you have Neptune aspecting the Nodes, your capacity for transcendent visions is particularly strong, and your relationship with that vision is especially intense. For you, it's Vision with a capital *V*. When this archetype is active, that Vision will be your inspiration, your guide, and your armor against all sorts of adversity, criticism, and disbelief. Of course, that same Vision may cause you to overlook very real obstacles in your path. Like Uranus, Neptune aspecting the Nodes gives you the opportunity to do things that are remarkable, unexpected, and maybe even magical, but it can also push you to do things that are reckless and unwise.

Visionaries

The archetypical figure for the visions of Neptune is, of course, the Visionary. And when you are discussing Visionaries, you almost have to start with the mystics.

In 1858, a teenage girl name Bernadette Soubirous (who had Neptune trine her South Node) was walking through the woods when she saw a woman in white surrounded by dazzling light. Bernadette knew immediately that it was the Virgin Mary stepping out of a grotto to have a conversation with her. At first, authorities in the Catholic Church doubted Bernadette's Vision, but the youngster held firm. She saw what she saw. Not only had she talked to the Virgin Mary, but now the spring that flowed from that cave was producing miraculous healings. Eventually, the Church dropped its objections and made Bernadette a saint. Unfortunately, by then the poor woman was dead.

Not every Neptunian Vision has to be mystical. Phyllis Schlafly, who had Neptune conjunct her North Node, gained national attention back in the 1970s when she led conservative opposition to the Equal Rights Amendment. She had a Vision of an America in which women were satisfied with their "traditional" role as subservient to and supportive of their husbands. After the Equal Rights Amendment was defeated, Schlafly became a fixture within the Republican Party, and she never wavered in her support for "family values." The critics who pointed out to Schlafly that her active public life did not fit her Vision of a woman's role were quickly dismissed. The Visionary has no time for such realistic details.

In direct opposition to Schlafly's Vision, we have the Vision that Hugh Hefner, who had Neptune quincunx the South Node, expressed in his Playboy philosophy. Hefner's Vision decried censorship and religious oppression. It replaced "family values" with the pleasure principle and called for sexual freedom for both men and women (though mostly for men). Hefner's Vision of the swinging bachelor was no more realistic or attainable than Schlafly's perfect little homemaker, but being unattainable is often part of the charm of a Neptunian Vision.

It is easy to see how Vision can apply to religion, politics, and philosophy, but it can also be important in more worldly affairs. Both Martha Stewart (with Neptune conjunct the North Node) and Oprah Winfrey (with the square) presented the world with a particular Vision of what people could do and be. Nikola Tesla (with Neptune quincunx the South Node) was a brilliant scientist and inventor, but he was also a Visionary. Likewise, we have three visionary businessmen, George Westinghouse, Ross Perot, and Henry Ford, all of whom had Neptune aspecting the Nodes of the Moon in their horoscopes.

Henry Ford, who had Neptune trine the North Node, was a man who had multiple Visions. His first was of a better way to build an automobile. That Vision made Ford a rich man. Ford also had a Vision of a well-paid workforce that would be loyal to his company, lead orderly lives (no drinking, church every Sunday), and make enough money to buy the cars they were manufacturing. This Vision also worked out well for Ford. Unfortunately, Ford had another Vision that was not nearly so productive. He believed that a secret Jewish cabal controlled international finance and much of the world's political structure. Since Ford also had Mercury aspecting the Nodes, he spent years disseminating his anti-Semitic rant through books and his own newspaper.

These examples illustrate some important points with regard to the visionary qualities of Neptune aspecting the Nodes. First of all, Neptunian Visions tend to come out of belief systems that are already deeply engrained. Bernadette was a devout Catholic living in a remote area of France. Given that background, her Vision of the Virgin Mary makes perfect sense. Secondly, Visions aren't susceptible to reality checks. The fact that Phyllis Schlafly spent far more time giving speeches, signing books, and participating in various conservative organizations than making breakfast for her husband had no bearing on her Vision of what a woman's life should be. Likewise, even though there was no factual basis for Henry Ford's theories of a Jewish conspiracy, the great industrialist was undeterred in his belief. This brings us to the third point: a Neptunian Visionary can create much that is good in the world and also much that is evil.

"Faith" versus "Vision"

In many ways, the Vision of people with Neptune aspecting the Nodes of the Moon resembles the faith of people with Jupiter aspecting the Nodes. Both demand a high level of commitment, and both can greatly alter and skew a person's view of reality. And yet, there is a difference in the way these two archetypes function. Even the most ardent of True Believers typically base their faith on some sort of rational argument or perceived reality. They've looked at their own lives and at the world and have seen a spiritual, political, or social need that their belief system addresses in a positive way. You can argue with a person with Jupiter aspecting the Nodes. You probably won't win, but you'll almost always learn something.

Arguing with a Neptunian Visionary, on the other hand, will most likely bring you nothing but frustration. Their Vision comes from a deeper, non-rational place. It will not be moved by debate or reason. The only thing that can change such a Vision is another visionary experience, and those don't come around very often.

We can see some of how this works in the life of Winston Churchill, who had Jupiter conjunct the South Node and Neptune conjunct his North Node. In chapter 7, I mentioned Churchill's prodigious alcohol intake. He also displayed Jupiterian improvidence in the handling of his money. Churchill had faith (well placed, as it turned out) that these deficiencies would never seriously hamper his health or his career. However, in terms of his politics, Churchill was not particularly faithful. He changed parties more than once. Churchill's political philosophy was based on his Vision of a great British Empire that spanned the globe. This Vision superseded the political concerns of the day as well as the arguments between left and right. That Vision was also the reason why Churchill refused to surrender to Hitler during the darkest days of World War II, even when many in his government thought the nation had no other choice. History is grateful to Winston Churchill for his stubborn commitment to his Vision.

Dreamers

While some people with Neptune aspecting the Nodes might be called Visionaries, others are more like Dreamers. Their visions are more personal, and often more commonplace. We might think of these Dreams as lacking the breadth and power of a Vision, but that's not always so. Martin Luther King Jr. (with Neptune square the Nodes) had a Dream that helped change the course of history.

Once upon a time, there was a girl named Chastity Bono, who dreamed that she might really be a boy. There was also a man named Bruce Jenner, who dreamed of himself as a woman. In another era, these two people would have been doomed to never see their dreams realized, but thanks to advances in medicine and changes in social attitudes, these two Dreamers were able to transition into their true gender. They are now known as Chaz Bono and Caitlyn Jenner.

Ed Wood Jr. had a Dream of becoming a great filmmaker, and, as Neptunian Dreamers often do, he devoted himself to making that Dream come true. With a minimal budget, amateurish special effects, and mostly untrained actors, he put together movies like *Plan Nine from Outer Space*, *Bride of the Monster*, and *Glen or Glenda*. None of Wood's films were very good. In fact, at one point, he was dubbed the worst filmmaker in the history of the medium. However, none of this detracted from the joy Wood found in making his movies. He was a Dreamer in pursuit of this Dream, and what could be more perfect than that.

There are, of course, other Dreamers with Neptune aspecting the Nodes who had more success. We have three famous poets—Percy Bysshe Shelley, Lord Byron, and William Wordsworth—known for their romantic imagery. We also have four novelists—Philip K. Dick, Hermann Hesse, Jorge Luis Borges, and Pamela Travers (author of *Mary Poppins*)—noted for their compelling fantasies.

Just having Neptune aspecting the Nodes of the Moon is not going to make you a great poet or novelist. However, creativity and imagination often accompany the Visionary experience. What you do with that creativity will depend on other factors in your horoscope, as well as on your training and education. But even if art, music, or poetry isn't your thing, you can still be a Dreamer. Your Dream might be of the perfect job, the perfect house, or the perfect lover. The fact that such dreams might seem unattainable is not a problem. The Dream is there to guide and inspire you and to keep you dreaming of greater things.

And Then Things Get Weird

The Visions and Dreams of Neptune aspecting the Lunar Nodes are not bound by reality. They are designed to exceed the possible and the mundane. This is why the Visionary and the Dreamer inspire us. There are times, though, when people with these aspects become so intent on following their Dreams and Visions that they do things and behave in ways that strike us as odd, unusual, or weird. It's not so much that these folks defy convention, as people with Uranus aspecting the Nodes might. It's more like they fail to recognize that these conventions exist.

Examples of this weirdness are not as common as Visionaries or Dreamers with Neptune aspecting the Nodes of the Moon, but they are striking. During the 1950s, Hollywood turned out a bevy of busty blonde actresses. However, only one of those bombshells regularly attended the bizarre satanic masses held by Anton LaVey and declared herself a Satanist. That was Jayne Mansfield, who had Neptune conjunct the North Node. Anton LaVey, by the way, has Neptune trine the North Node.

It's not that uncommon for rock 'n' roll stars to have disputes with their record companies. Only one resolved his disagreement by changing his name to an unpronounceable symbol and referring to himself as "the artist formerly known as Prince." Prince had Neptune conjunct the North Node. David Bowie, who had Neptune trine the North Node, might have started the trend of dolling himself up with heavy makeup and assuming an alternate persona, but no one took that trend farther than Kiss's Gene Simmons, who had Neptune conjunct the North Node.

Not everyone with Neptune aspecting the Nodes of the Moon enjoys being labeled as "weird." Bela Lugosi, who had Neptune conjunct the South Node, was a classically trained actor, but once he played Dracula, he was limited to playing similarly bizarre and creepy characters for the rest of his career. Also, the weirdness of Neptune can sometimes take an ugly turn, veering away from benign oddity and careening into scandal. Examples of this include Linda Tripp and Paula Jones, both with Neptune on the South Node and both of whom became entangled in the scandal involving Bill Clinton and Monica Lewinsky.

As I said at the beginning of this chapter, Neptune identity is amorphous. It defies clear definition. Dreams and Visions can take you in many different directions. So can weirdness. The faces that the Neptunian archetype shows us are often hard to define and prone to blend and blur, one into another.

Substance Abuse

Neptune can represent the need to find a higher spiritual truth. It can also be the source of great creativity and visionary ideas. However, Neptune obliterates boundaries, and without boundaries, human beings can quickly go astray. One way this can happen is through addiction and substance abuse.

We saw examples of this with Jupiter aspecting the Nodes. We see about the same amount with Neptune. The horoscopes of these examples typically show either Neptune or Jupiter aspecting one of the personal planets as well. In other words, this face of the archetype found an environment conducive to this manifestation. One way in which the people with Neptune aspecting the Nodes seem to be different is that, for them, the drinking and drugging is less a matter of lifestyle (as it often seems to be with Jupiter aspecting the Nodes) and more an interruption or diversion of their larger vision. Still, even though anyone with Neptune prominent in their chart in any way has to be mindful of these issues, a proper judgment regarding addiction and drug or alcohol abuse can only be made after a consideration of the entire horoscope.

The Archetype and You

More than any other planet, Neptune is associated with spirituality and mysticism. From this, we might assume that if you were born with Neptune aspecting the Nodes of the Moon, you have a special relationship with fate, karma, and the great mysteries of the universe. You understand that there is more to life than what is available to our physical senses or our intellect.

You recognize the importance of aligning your desires with forces beyond the material world. For you, Dreams and Visions are not just products of imagination. They are your means of entering the flow of the universe.

From this, it might be assumed that people born with Neptune aspecting the Nodes came out of a past life in which they were deeply spiritual, and that this has left them with a greater respect for the power of Vision and Dreams. It could also be that in a past life, their dreams were curtailed or crushed and, in this life, they have the opportunity to experience them to the fullest. On the other hand, we could take a more prosaic approach. Maybe the Dreams and Visions that people with these aspects have are merely extensions of what they did in a past life. Maybe Ed Wood Jr. was a great movie or theater director in a past life and Phyllis Schlafly was a meek and contented housewife.

If you have Neptune aspecting the Nodes, you "see" where you want to go and what you want to accomplish before (sometimes long before) the work toward those goals begins. You are not so much driven as drawn toward your goals. You are drawn toward them because they feel right to you, because your Vision has told you that this is where you were meant to be.

This might seem rather silly to the more practical side of your personality. Some of you might deny ever having such visionary experiences. That's because this archetype has not yet found a comfortable place to land in your personality. Maybe it never will. Maybe your cynicism is too deep to allow the Visionary or the Dreamer to come to the surface. Or maybe you shy away from this archetype because it has led you astray in a previous life. Certainly, there are many good reasons for not giving in to the dreamy alure of Neptune. In fact, there is only one reason why you should consider following the Dreams and Visions this archetype brings you—you need them to feel fully alive.

If you have Neptune aspecting the Nodes, it is your Vision that will lift your life from the commonplace and add purpose and meaning to your existence. It makes no difference if your Vision shows you the mother of God or a better way of assembling an automobile; you see it, and you know that it is true. This is by no means a guarantee that what you've visualized will become a reality, but that's not what's important. What's important is the way that Vision, that Dream, inspires and energizes you.

109

Of course, as we have seen, some Visions are more worthwhile than others, and some can be hateful and destructive. If you have Neptune aspecting the Nodes of the Moon, you will likely be called upon at some point in your life to dream big, to visualize what might seem impossible, unprovable, and irrational. That's fine, but you have to be sure that those big dreams are positive and productive, that they broaden your perspective and deepen your understanding of the world. Because the thing about Dreams and Visions is that even the ones that seem impossible sometimes come true, and if that happens, you want your Vision to be one of which you can truly be proud.

CHAPTER 12

Pluto Aspecting the North or South Nodes

Yeah, I know. Why would I be writing about Pluto? Everybody knows that it's not a planet anymore. My answer to that is this. Before 2006, astronomers did not have clear definitions of what a planet was, so they created one that satisfied the physical criteria that interested them. That definition excluded Pluto. Astrologers have always known the definition of a planet. It is a body in the solar system that has relevance to human affairs here on Earth. The discovery of Pluto in 1930 roughly coincided with the rise of fascism, the rise of communism, World War II, the Holocaust, and the dropping of the first atomic bomb. This was Pluto's entrance into our consciousness, and you have to admit, it was a darned impressive entrance. I see all that as evidence that Pluto has relevance to human affairs. Therefore, as far as astrology is concerned, Pluto is still a planet.

Those events I just listed have given Pluto a reputation as an astrological tough guy. Even though modern astrologers generally shy away from the idea of "good" and "bad" planets, Pluto seems to have joined Mars and Saturn, the two "malefics" of traditional astrology, as one of the solar system's villains. I'm not so sure about this. My observation of Pluto in the horoscope is that it is by no means always "bad." However, it is always serious. Any time you are dealing with Pluto, you have to dispense with the levity (unless you like gallows humor) and focus. You have to be prepared to deal with fundamental issues. You have to be prepared for transformation.

Transformation

What is transformation? Let's start with what it is not. It is not change. If you decide to dump your high school sweetheart in order to go out with a new guy who seems more exciting, that's change. If the new guy turns out to be a dud, there's always a chance that you can go back to your old boyfriend. He may not be particularly happy with you, but he's still there.

With the kind of transformation that Pluto brings into our lives, there is no turning back. That's because whatever you left behind is no longer there or no longer has meaning to you. This is what makes encounters with Pluto so serious. For better or worse, they give us no choice but to go forward. Often these transformations are forced upon us by situations over which we have no control. It might be the death of a loved one, a catastrophic weather event, or a sudden change in the economic or political environment. On the other hand, Pluto can also bring us transformations that are quiet and incremental. You wake up one day and realize that over a period of months or even years you have outgrown some part of your identity or a particular relationship. When did this happen? You don't exactly know, but you do know that you can never go back.

As an archetype for this sort of transformation, we probably couldn't do much better than the deity for which this planet was named. Pluto was the god of the underworld and the god of death, which is the most profound transformation of them all. That makes this dusty old Roman god an apt representative for this deep and meaningful process.

It's probably safe to say that everyone goes through at least one of these transformative events in the course of their lifetime. However, for the person with Pluto aspecting the Nodes, these transformative experiences carry extra weight. Many astrologers, and particularly those in the Evolutionary School, link Pluto to reincarnation and fate. You know things are serious when there is more than one incarnation involved. And even without this connection to past lives, it is the function of Pluto to take us down to the most basic level of our existence, to a place where our awareness of the day-to-day realities dim while our understanding of a broader and more essential reality becomes sharper. It makes no difference whether you relate this deeper awareness to reincarnation or to a psychological complex; it can be a vehicle for profound, life-changing transformation.

Transformation through Events

Simon Wiesenthal, who was born with Pluto conjunct the North Node, had no control over the event that completely transformed his life. That was the German invasion of Poland in 1939. Once the Nazis were in control, as a Jew, Wiesenthal immediately became a victim. He and his wife were sent to concentration camps. Many of his relatives were killed. Wiesenthal survived the Holocaust and devoted the rest of his life to hunting down fugitive Nazis all around the world.

We humans tend to assume that we have things under control, that our plans and aspirations matter. Pluto comes along and shows us otherwise, often in dramatic fashion. Part of Pluto's function in the horoscope is to expose our hubris, to blast away our silly, prideful notions of ego and autonomy and make us truly aware of our cosmic insignificance. However, at the same time, Pluto also reminds us of the resilience and capacity for renewal that resides at the deepest levels of every human heart. Yes, we may not be a match for the vast forces arrayed against us, but, even in the most impossible circumstances, we can survive.

For an unemployed traveling salesman named Adolf Eichmann, who had Pluto trine the South Node, the same events that put Simon Wiesenthal in a concentration camp became a transformative career opportunity. He joined the SS and, since Eichmann had picked up a smattering of Yiddish during his travels, he was quickly dubbed an "expert" on the "Jewish question" and promoted.

Meanwhile, in France, the life of a brilliant young philosopher and mystic named Simone Weil, who had Pluto conjunct the North Node, was being transformed in a different way. When Germany invaded France, Weil fled with her parents to the United States, but she returned to England, determined to fight alongside the Free French against the Nazis. When her poor health made this impossible, Weil refused to eat more than what she reasoned the French people living under German occupation were eating. It is generally thought that her self-starvation contributed to the philosopher's untimely death in 1943.

We are all subject to the whims of history and great events that punctuate the times in which we live. Often those events overpower us, cause us to change our plans, and postpone our aspirations. For people with Pluto aspecting the Lunar Nodes, however, these changes can have a transformative effect, and that transformation often has something to do with power.

While he was a prisoner of the Nazis, Simon Wiesenthal was deprived of any vestige of personal power. After World War II, he sought to avenge his suffering and the suffering of so many others. As the world's most famous "Nazi hunter," Wiesenthal became the one with the power: the power of vengeance. For Adolf Eichmann, on the other hand, the Nazi period gave him the power of life or death over hundreds of thousands of people. The end of the war, of course, stripped that power away and made him a fugitive.

Simone Weil never suffered the cruelties of a concentration camp. Her experience of Pluto's power was indirect, and yet it was no less real. It is often the case that people under the influence of this guest feel desperate and develop a fixity of purpose that can seem obsessive. Much depends on what else is happening in the horoscope, and Weil possessed a personality already inclined toward intensity. Deprived by her illness of a means of reasserting her will, Weil took desperate measures. She looked to the few things she could control. One of them was how much she ate.

The resemblance between the Roman god of the dead and the Christian concept of Satan is not an accident. They both represent the same dark and mysterious archetype. Like Satan, Pluto tempts us, not with physical pleasure or earthly glory, but with power. This might be power over other people, or power over your own physical or social limitations, or even power over fate. For people with Pluto aspecting the Nodes of the Moon, this temptation can be especially hard to resist, and for many of them, it turns out to be a devil's bargain.

Quiet Transformations

It is fairly easy to find people with Pluto aspecting the Nodes of the Moon whose lives were transformed by events in the public sphere. After all, those transformations often make the news. Rodney King (with Pluto square the Nodes) had his life transformed when he was stopped and beaten by Los Angeles police. Christopher Reeve's (with Pluto on the South Node) was tragically transformed by a horseback riding accident. Jacqueline Kennedy Onassis's (with Pluto trine the South Node) transformation came after her husband was assassinated. However, transformation that involves private and personal issues can be just as important.

These quiet transformations are often slow and incremental. They may go unrecognized by the outside world. You may not be totally aware of them yourself, and, even if you are, you may have trouble conceptualizing what is happening. Pluto works at a level in our psyche that often defies both rational explanation and emotional understanding. It's only when you're faced with the results, for better or worse, that the fundamental nature of the change becomes clear.

In 1979, FBI agent Robert Hanssen decided to start selling secret documents to the Russians. This transformative decision was not made for ideological or political reasons. Hanssen claimed that he just wanted to make some money. It is also likely that stealing secrets from under the noses of his bosses at the FBI and selling them to the Soviets gave Hanssen a sense of power. It validated his belief that he was smarter than his peers at the Bureau. Nonetheless, the transformation of this trusted agent into a spy went unnoticed for over twenty years.

Sometimes astrology can give us a clue as to when and how these internal transformations might happen. In 1945, the young woman named Norma Jeane Mortenson was a married factory worker who did a little modeling on the side. By the end of 1946, she divorced her husband, signed with a modeling agency, got a contract with 20th Century Fox, and changed her name to Marilyn Monroe. What brought about this transformation? One thing that we know is that during this period, transiting Pluto was making an important contact with her horoscope. Quite literally (in an astrological sense, anyway), Marilyn was visited by Pluto.

The transformation of Norma Jeane Mortenson into Marilyn Monroe was fairly quick by Pluto standards. More often, the internal transformations this archetype brings us are much more gradual. They cannot be tied to any one transit. The transformation of George William Jorgensen Jr. into Christine Jorgensen seems to have covered several years. From her school days on into her young adulthood, Jorgensen (who had Pluto conjunct the North Node) struggled with a sense of being the wrong gender. As a child, she was bullied because of her effeminate manner, and she learned to conceal both her femininity and her sexual attraction to boys. However, the sense that something wasn't right continued to haunt her.

Jorgensen was born at a time when problems of gender identity were not understood. To some extent, they were not even considered to be a possibility. It took years for Jorgensen to recognize both her problem and that there was something she could do about it. Jorgensen was twenty-four when she decided to travel to Europe to find a doctor who would help her transition. Even after this was accomplished, her physical transformation went through several phases and was not completed until four years later.

Pluto doesn't so much enter our life as cast a shadow over it. Sometimes it is easy to identify the source of that shadow. It's a war, a recession, a diagnosis, or an injury. Other times, the shadow seems to come from inside us, and we are only able to identify its source after intense self-examination. However, whether the process is sudden or slow, the goal is always the same: Pluto brings us transformation. It may not be the transformation that we want, but it is almost always a transformation that we need.

Zeitgeist

It is interesting how often you find names that seem essential to the zeitgeist of a particular period of history or culture when you look down a list of people born with Pluto aspecting the Nodes. Think of Marilyn Monroe and the 1950s. Alongside her, you might put Joseph McCarthy, who had Pluto conjunct the North Node. How could you think of the age of invention in America and not think of Thomas Edison, who had Pluto conjunct the South Node? How can you talk about the late twentieth century and not mention the movies of Steven Spielberg?

This connection between individuals with these aspects and their times is not always positive. Bernie Madoff, with Pluto trine the North Node, has come to represent the rampant greed that eventually led to the Great Recession of 2008. The tumult of the 1960s was helped along by three assassins— Lee Harvey Oswald, Sirhan Sirhan, and James Earl Ray—all of whom had Pluto aspecting the Nodes.

For many of these people with Pluto aspecting the Lunar Nodes, the connection to the times in which they lived had to do with power. This is certainly true for Vladimir Putin and Indira Gandhi, both with Pluto conjunct the South Node. But you don't have to be the leader of a country or even famous for this connection to ring true. Maybe you're someone who identifies closely with the zeitgeist of your times, or maybe you are someone who profited or suffered in a very unique and specific way because of times into which you happened to be born. As with everything involving Pluto, the importance of this connection might not be readily apparent. It resides somewhere deep in your consciousness.

The Archetype and You

Not everything is gloom and doom with Pluto aspecting the Lunar Nodes. There are some stories that are quite positive and even inspirational. The transformation that occurred in the life of the Scottish singer named Susan Boyle (with Pluto conjunct her North Node) when she sang "I Dreamed a Dream" on *Britain's Got Talent* worked out pretty well. The same could be said for what happened to Oprah Winfrey (with Pluto quincunx the North Node) after the popularity of her syndicated talk show transformed her into one of those rare people with whom the world is on a first-name basis. Robert Downey Jr. (with the square) transformed himself from a helpless addict into one of Hollywood's highest-paid stars. We can hope that the transformation of Britain's Prince Harry (with Pluto quincunx the North Node) from a royal to a nonroyal will serve him well.

However, even when the transformation that Pluto aspecting the Nodes brings into your life is positive, it is still serious business, and you have to be prepared to deal with it in a serious way. You have to expect that this transformation is going to bring out issues with regard to your character and your psyche that you have either previously ignored or just don't like looking at. You have to expect to be made uncomfortable and to be challenged in a substantial way. That's because Pluto changes us in fundamental ways.

The transformations that people with these aspects go through are often accompanied by a loss. It might be the loss of a job, or a loved one, or of money and prestige. Again, that is what's on the surface. No matter how significant that loss is to your material circumstance, its real importance is how it transforms you on a deeper psychological and spiritual level. You may not recognize the true extent of this transformation until months or even years after the grief over your loss has passed.

One of the most common things you lose when this archetypical visitor is active in your life is your pride, your power, and your sense of autonomy. This is a necessary part of the process. Pluto demands that you see yourselves as you really are. It's not what's on your resumé, and it's not what's on your Tinder profile. It is who you are, stripped of your illusions and deprived of your self-pity. Pluto takes you down to your most basic components, to the things about you that will endure and serve as the building blocks for the new you who will come out of this transformation.

In terms of reincarnation, some people might think that people suffering through a particularly difficult Pluto transformation are getting paid back for bad behavior in a past life. However, there are other options. It could be that having Pluto aspecting the Nodes of the Moon signals the need for an adjustment, a correction to the trajectory of your spiritual journey. Both the big, transformative events and the slow, incremental transformations are there to reset your course and prepare you for the next leg of your soul's odyssey. Some pain might be necessary. There might also be frustration and loss. But the ultimate goal is to get to where you need to be. Whether you will accomplish that goal in this life or another is something we cannot know.

When you feel this guest sitting beside you, it might be tempting to take your hands off the wheel and leave the driving to the powers that be, whether they are political, economic, or spiritual. And yet, your intention, your awareness, and your struggle are also an important part of this process. You have to offer them up, even if it is as a sacrifice. You have to go until you hit the limits of your agency, until the irresistible wave finally swallows you up. That's when you know that the transformation is complete—not when you've given up, but when you've given all you have to give.

The other thing you need to be mindful of when Pluto aspecting the Nodes is asserting its influence is holding on to your compassion. It is very easy when you are struggling with your inner demons or under the thumb of oppressive circumstances to assume that it's all about you. You get lost in your own self-examination and in your own trials and victories. You have to remember that there are a lot of people with Pluto aspecting the Lunar Nodes. Given the duration of Pluto aspecting the Nodes, quite a few of them were probably born around the same time as you. Also, Pluto brings transformation to everyone at one time or another, even those who do not share these aspects to the Lunar Nodes. You have to find time in your struggle and room in your heart for these other people. Your familiarity with this archetype, unpleasant as it might be, gives you the opportunity to advise and guide those with less experience. It gives you a chance to share your wisdom.

And you will have wisdom to give. In many ways, the ultimate goal of every Pluto transformation is a step forward in terms of self-awareness, character, and wisdom. People with these aspects, particularly the ones who have experienced the full force of Pluto, frequently have a perspective on life and a depth of understanding that is far beyond the ordinary. They are less fearful of life's little bumps and bruises and more forgiving of the foibles and errors of their fellow human beings. This is how Pluto gives us back the power it had once taken away, and this is power that will forever be ours, through this lifetime and whatever comes after.

PART
TWO

Now it's time to get technical. Understanding the meaning of aspects by the Sun, Moon, and planets to the Lunar Nodes is an important first step, but it is still only a first step. The ultimate goal is always integrating this knowledge into a complete understanding of a person's horoscope. In this section of the book, we will examine a few celebrity horoscopes in depth, looking at how aspects to the Nodes of the Moon work within the totality of the chart. We will see how an aspect to the Nodes can be subdued in the life of one person and become explosively obvious in another.

We will also explore specific issues involving aspects to the Lunar Nodes, such as how to deal with multiple aspects to the Nodes and what it means to have no aspects to the Nodes. In chapter 16, we will leave aspects behind and examine the house placements and sign placements of the Lunar Nodes. In chapter 17, we will briefly discuss transiting aspects involving the Nodes of the Moon.

While we're dealing with technical issues, we also need to consider the motion of the Nodes of the Moon around the ecliptic. There are two ways of measuring that movement. The first is called the True Node. Computers now allow us to track minute fluctuations in the movement of the Lunar Nodes, and it turns out that they move in a herky-jerky, back-and-forth manner. The other is the Mean Node. This is an average of the movement of the Node during a twenty-four-hour period. My preference is the Mean Node. I feel that, since we're dealing with an abstract, mathematical point and not a physical body, a mathematical approximation is sufficient. I've been told that the difference between the Mean and True Node can be up to 4 degrees. However, in my own experience, I have yet to see a difference of more than 2 degrees.

Readers who have only a minimal knowledge of astrology might see this section as being only for the "experts," but every astrology book should give people the opportunity to expand their knowledge of this fascinating and complex subject. Readers who prefer a more basic approach may go to part 3, where I have provided lists that contain a simplified summary of all these factors.

CHAPTER 13

Working with Aspects to the Nodes

The first thing you have to do when working with aspects to the Nodes of the Moon is forget about them, at least for a while. That might seem impossible once you are aware of what they can do, but you can't really know how these aspects are going to function in a horoscope until you understand the personality that horoscope describes. I call these aspects guests, visitors, and hidden influencers, because they are not really part of what we understand as the basic personality. They come into our lives from another place, and how they impact us depends on the traits and tendencies that are already hardwired into our nature.

In order to better understand how this process works, let's look at some sample horoscopes. We'll start with the chart of singer Karen Carpenter.

The information about Carpenter's life comes from Randy Schmidt's 2010 biography, *Little Girl Blue: The Life of Karen Carpenter*.

At first glance, the indicators for success in Carpenter's chart seem quite obvious. We have the Sun in the Tenth House of career, Uranus conjunct the Ascendant, and the Moon in Leo. This describes an ambitious person with a unique personality who gets emotional satisfaction from pleasing an audience.

It would be hard to imagine a better horoscope for a performer. However, Carpenter grew up with the notion that she was not supposed to be successful. It was her brother Richard who was the musical genius, and it was toward advancing his career that Carpenter's middle-class parents devoted their financial and emotional resources. Karen was just the tagalong little sister. Richard let her accompany him as a drummer and occasionally asked her to sing the songs he wrote and arranged.

Looking at the horoscope a little closer, we see that Carpenter's ambitious Sun in the Tenth House is in Pisces, a sign that can be highly creative but also is inclined toward passivity. On top of this, the Sun is opposed to Saturn, which is placed in the Fourth House of home. This clearly describes Tenth House ambition and hunger for recognition being held back by restrictive influences coming out of the person's home environment.

The placement of the Moon in Carpenter's chart also plays a part in this conflict. Her Leo Moon is in the Third House opposed to Jupiter. Carpenter's emotional security was very much tied to routines of her immediate environment and, from her childhood on, that routine was built around the idea that Richard was the talented one. The opposition to Jupiter called for an expansion of that narrow point of view, but Carpenter's Moon is also conjunct Pluto, which deepens the sensitivity that is always a part of the Moon's function and adds qualities of fear and obsession. Even though Jupiter is helped by a conjunction to Mercury, the task of lifting Carpenter out of the emotionally "safe" routines of being just another supportive fan of her brilliant brother and toward a broader and more rational view of the world was seriously impeded from the start.

To all of this, we add Mars conjunct the South Node of the Moon. The archetype is the Warrior, but there is little room in the personality described by Karen Carpenter's horoscope for a Warrior. At various times in Carpenter's life, it appears that the Warrior tried to emerge. More than once she moved out of the home she shared with her mother and tried to live on her own, but she always returned. At one point, Carpenter rebelled and made an album with a producer other than her brother, only to have Richard refuse to let their record company release it.

Meanwhile, the brother and sister team called The Carpenters produced hit record after hit record. Karen's soulful renditions of Richard's arrangements (evidence of both her Pisces Sun and Cancer Ascendant) made her one of the most beloved singers of the 1970s. Her voice was unique, just as we might expect of a singer with Uranus on the Ascendant, and Carpenter had all the success in her career that her Tenth House Sun predicted. But what about Mars on her South Node? What about the Warrior? In Carpenter's chart, Mars is weak by sign (in Libra), and the conjunction of her Moon to Pluto made it easy for Karen to internalize this archetype's influence. Instead of fighting to free herself from the restrictions imposed on her by her family and her own passivity, Carpenter went to war with herself. She developed anorexia and, over time, tragically starved herself to death.

For a better outcome with Mars aspecting the Lunar Nodes, we can take a look at the horoscope of Whoopi Goldberg.

Here we have a chart with both the Sun and Moon, along with Mercury and Saturn, in Scorpio. They form a stellum in Goldberg's Ninth House, which has to do with religion, philosophy, and the higher mind. This describes a deep thinker and a person with very strong opinions. This tendency is reinforced by the fact that she has Aquarius rising.

The traditional ruler of Scorpio is Mars and, even though this sign doesn't have the combative reputation of Aries, Scorpio people also appreciate the thrill of a good fight now and then. However, Scorpios typically prefer to keep their aggressive intentions hidden. They favor an indirect attack, and their weapons of choice are sarcasm and backhanded insults. With Scorpio, you often don't realize that you've been burned until long after the Scorpio has left the room.

In Karen Carpenter's chart, the Sun was opposed by Saturn. The Sun is conjunct Saturn in Goldberg's. A conjunction to Saturn works differently from an opposition. While an opposition to Saturn blocks and obstructs, a conjunction combines Saturn's practicality, discipline, and need for firm boundaries with the attributes of the planet with which it is aligned. Saturn conjunct Goldberg's Scorpio Sun doesn't so much impede that sign's aggressive potential as make it more circumspect and purposeful. Goldberg likes to pick her battles and know the ground on which she is fighting.

Unfortunately for Goldberg, Mars in her chart is not strong. It is placed in Libra (as was Karen Carpenter's Mars) and in the Eighth House. Mars in Libra is considered in its "detriment" or at its weakest, while Mars in the Eighth House personalizes Goldberg's anger. When the fighter in Goldberg is activated, her responses are often based on her own experiences and emotional baggage rather than on ideas or principles. During her career, Goldberg has been criticized for her stubborn defense of Bill Cosby and Mel Gibson in the face of powerful evidence of their misbehavior. Goldberg's support was apparently based on her personal interactions with these men.

Still, despite these criticisms, Goldberg has never shown any inclination to withhold her opinions. As the longtime host of the television talk show *The View*, Goldberg has literally made a living out of expressing her strong and often controversial opinions on current affairs and politics. This might not be something we would expect from a person with Mars so weakly placed, but in Goldberg's horoscope, Mars is also trine the South Node of the Moon. After a long and stellar career as a comedian, then as an actress, then as a businessperson, the Warrior visited Whoopi Goldberg, and, at least as this is being written, it still holds a place in her psyche.

In Goldberg's Scorpio-dominated horoscope, the Warrior found an environment that was much more conducive to its nature than what we saw in the horoscope of Karen Carpenter. Another factor in the Warrior's favor is the fact that Goldberg's Sun and Moon are in the Ninth House. It isn't just about aggression for Goldberg. With the Sun and Moon in the Ninth, she feels the need to express her opinions, ideals, and principles to the world. She is a bit of a preacher, and this also fits into the agenda of the Warrior quite well.

The horoscopes of Karen Carpenter and Whoopi Goldberg clearly show us how the personality described by the horoscope determines the way in which a planet aspecting the Nodes will function. They demonstrate how that personality can hide or redirect the archetype represented by the aspecting planet or give it emphasis. However, it might also be interesting to look at a chart in which the archetype is so well received that its influence becomes overwhelming.

There is no doubt that Julian Assange is a Warrior.

From his boyhood on, he has done battle with the too big and the too powerful. The battle began when Assange was still a teenager living in Australia and he hacked a large communications company there. Then he moved to Europe where he helped found Wikileaks and devoted himself to publishing secret documents that revealed the clandestine activities of large institutions and governments. Often these documents also revealed abuses and crimes committed by dictatorships and oppressive governments. This made Assange a hero to many people, particularly those who leaned toward the political left. Then, in 2010, Wikileaks released material related to US military operations around the world that had been illegally obtained by Chelsea Manning. This put Assange at odds with the United States government and led to an investigation by the US Department of Justice.

There is also no doubt among astrologers about why Assange is such a Warrior. Mars is angular in his horoscope, within 2 degrees of a conjunction to the imum coeli (IC; "bottom of the sky"), the point directly opposite the midheaven. This placement gives Mars enormous power within his personality. Even though Assange's chart is primarily a water sign chart, with the Sun in Cancer and the Moon in Scorpio, Mars speaks with a very loud voice. Assange's Mars is in Aquarius, so it presents as the principled Warrior, a fighter driven by his ideals. This quality is furthered by the fact that Assange's Sun is square Uranus. Along with being a fighter, Assange is a rebel, a man who holds his principles above the commonplace restrictions of conventional morality.

Mars may speak loudly in Assange's horoscope, but it is not the only voice. The water sign placement of both his Sun and Moon shows us that emotion plays a huge role in his decisions and point of view. The houses occupied by Assange's Sun and Moon augment this tendency. His Sun is in the Eighth House, which often conveys an obsession with power, while his Moon is in the Twelfth, which can indicate an obsession with secrecy. The combination of house position, particularly with a water sign Sun and Moon, describes a loner and a person caught up in fighting his own inner demons. No matter what the principled Warrior in Assange's nature calls for, the battle for him is always going to revolve around personal issues. The intellectual purity of Aquarius and Uranus stands little chance in this horoscope.

Into this personality, we bring the North Node of the Moon, which is conjunct both Assange's Mars and his IC. Not only is Julian Assange a warrior, but he is also a Warrior, and this archetype hasn't just found an agreeable environment in Assange's horoscope—it has found a paradise. It would be difficult to say where the influence of Mars on his basic personality stops and the archetype of the Warrior begins. However, there can be no doubt that having both Mars conjunct the North Node and his IC has played an extensive role in Assange's life.

In 2010, a charge of sexual assault caused Julian Assange to take refuge in the Ecuadorian embassy in London. While he was living in the embassy, Wikileaks published material hacked by Russian agents from the computer of the Democratic National Committee. Since these publications were seen as helping a conservative Republican named Donald Trump get elected as president of the United States, Assange's status as a hero of the left was somewhat tarnished. This didn't seem to bother Assange. When he was finally kicked out of the Ecuadorian embassy in 2017, Assange was indicted in the United States for his activities with Chelsea Manning. In January 2021, a British judge ruled that Assange could not be extradited to stand trial in the United States. The United States has appealed this verdict, and the status of that appeal, as of this writing, has yet to be decided.

Mars conjunct the North Node hit the horoscope of Julian Assange like gasoline hitting a fire. It made a man already predisposed to fight any perceived injustice into a Warrior who can't seem to find a way to stop fighting. It is easy to see Assange as coming out of a past life in which he was badly treated by figures of authority and as a person who now feels compelled in this life to right those wrongs. But, regardless of how or why Assange took on the role of the Warrior, the battle has not gone well for him. It caused him to live for seven years as an increasingly less-than-honored guest of the Ecuadorian government with the displeasure of the governments of both the

United Kingdom and the United States hanging over him. It got him arrested and jailed by British authorities, with the possibility of much more serious legal problems in the United States looming in his future.

These examples show three ways in which one of these archetypical figures can interact with the personality that is described in the horoscope. There are many other possible scenarios, and that's just with Mars. Describing all the different possibilities for the Sun, the Moon, and the eight planets would, of course, be impossible. However, it is possible to point out some basic factors in the horoscope that could help or hinder the influence of these archetypes. In part 3, you will find a list of these factors.

CHAPTER 14

Multiple Aspects
to the Nodes

In chapter 1, I explained what an aspect was, but I didn't discuss orbs. The orb of an aspect refers to the exact distance (by degree and minute) that is allowable for that aspect to be effective. There are no hard-and-fast rules about orbs. Some astrologers favor wider orbs than others, and most use different orbs depending on what type of astrology they're doing. For example, the orb allowed from an aspect in a natal horoscope might be 5 degrees, while in the horoscope for an event, an orb of only 1 or 2 degrees would be applicable.

The orbs I used in my study of aspects to the Nodes of the Moon are as follows: 5 degrees 59 minutes for the conjunctions, 3 degrees 30 minutes for squares and trines, 1 degree 30 minutes for quincunxes. With the Lunar Nodes, any consideration of aspects is complicated by the fact that there are two of them and they are always 180 degrees apart. That means that every conjunction to one Node is an opposition to the other, every square to one is a square to the other, every trine to one is a sextile to the other, and every quincunx to one is a semi-sextile to the other. I focused on the conjunction, square, trine, and quincunx because I felt they were the stronger aspects.

For the sake of simplicity, I used the same orb when the aspect was apply-ing (getting closer) and separating (moving apart), and I applied these orbs strictly to every aspect to the Nodes for every example I've cited.

Using these orbs (which are relatively tight), it is common for people to have more than one planet aspecting the Nodes of the Moon. In fact, it would seem that most people have multiple aspects to the Nodes. The norm appears to be at least three while some people have as many as five or six. This is why some of the celebrity examples were mentioned in more than one chapter. Each of these multiple archetypes can make itself felt in the per-son's life in a different way.

One of those people who got mentioned in more than one chapter is Marilyn Monroe. She is mentioned in chapters 4, 9, and 12.

Monroe actually had four aspects to her North Node. The Moon was quincunx, Mars and Saturn were trine, and Pluto was conjunct. Each of these archetypical visitors contributed to a different portion of Monroe's life story. In chapter 12, I discussed how she transformed herself from a newly married fac-tory worker named Norma Jeane Mortenson into the actress named Marilyn Monroe. This was Pluto's work. Then Mars took over. Marilyn competed. She took acting lessons, she slept with producers, she did whatever she needed to do to get ahead. And then the Moon stepped in. Because of the vulnerability she was able to project on the screen, Marilyn Monroe became not just famous, but an icon. This fame brought Saturn and doubt into the picture, which resulted in increasing insecurity, erratic behavior, failed marriages, and addiction.

Normally, we would think that some aspects to the Nodes would be more powerful than others. If we were to put the aspects that Monroe had to her Nodes in the context for a typical horoscope reading, we would probably put the conjunction to Pluto first in terms of influence, then the trines, and the quincunx to the Moon last. However, with aspects to the Nodes, this hierarchy doesn't seem to apply. In fact, considering Monroe's enduring fame, it would seem that it is the quincunx that is primary.

Another interesting feature of these aspects to the Nodes is how they seem to show up at specific times in the person's life and then fade away. This is tragically evident in the case of Marilyn Monroe. Where was the transformative energy of Pluto late in Monroe's life when she was struggling with addiction? Where was the competitive Warrior when her erratic behavior began to eat away at her career? Why did it seem that, in the last years of Monroe's life, the only archetypes she was listening to were doubting Saturn and the vulnerable Moon?

This is where we have to consider the horoscope as a whole. In Marilyn Monroe's natal horoscope, Saturn was square the Moon. This aspect was part of a T square that also involved Neptune and Jupiter. These aspects describe both Monroe's absent mother and her needy emotional nature. They also provided for a personality in which both the vulnerability of the Moon and Saturn's doubt could easily find space. In judging the influence of aspects to the Nodes of the Moon, it is not the type of aspect that is important; it is the personality described by everything else in the horoscope. In the case of Marilyn Monroe, that personality provided an environment that was more friendly to the Moon and Saturn than it was to Pluto and Mars. The last two archetypes had some impact during specific periods of Monroe's life, but they faded as Saturn and the Moon gained ground.

Monroe's chart illustrates another common feature of multiple aspects to the Nodes. If more than one planet is aspecting the Lunar Nodes, those planets will frequently be aspecting one another in the natal chart. Another example of this is the filmmaker Michael Moore.

In Moore's chart, we have two planets aspecting the Nodes. Uranus is conjunct the South Node of the Moon and Mercury is square. As you might expect, Mercury and Uranus are themselves in a 90-degree aspect.

I don't think there's any doubt that, as a maker of documentary films, Michael Moore fits into the archetype of the Messenger. There is also no doubt that his work often has a mischievous edge. In films like *Bowling for Columbine* and *Capitalism: A Love Story*, Moore delivers a powerful message that is designed to get under the skin of certain groups of people. It isn't just about the message. Moore often films himself playing the part of the Trickster and doing things like disrupting a GM stockholder meeting or putting police tape around the building that housed Goldman Sachs. Mercury in Moore's chart is in his Ninth House along with his Sun, placements that augment the archetype of the Messenger. Meanwhile, Uranus and the Trickster bring in the perfect complement to the message that Mercury seeks to deliver.

In Moore's chart, there is natural symbiosis between the Messenger and the Trickster. That is not the case with every combination. For example, what would happen if you added the archetype of the Moon to a horoscope with Mercury and Uranus aspecting the Lunar Nodes?

The author H. P. Lovecraft was born with Mercury square the Nodes and the Moon and Uranus trine the North Node.

In his chart, the Moon and Uranus are conjunct. The aspect between Mercury and Uranus is a weak semi-sextile.

Lovecraft's personality was rife with contradictions. He was a lover of classic literature and a prolific writer of pulp fiction. He was a xenophobic nativist who married a foreign-born Jew. He was a proud and independent Sun-sign Leo who lived with his mother until he was twenty-nine. He was an antisocial curmudgeon who maintained a wide network of correspondents and friends. These contradictions are described in Lovecraft's horoscope, but they also reflect the influence of the three planets aspecting his Nodes.

As a Messenger, few writers have had more to say than H. P. Lovecraft. Along with the tales of horror and the supernatural for which he is famous, Lovecraft wrote a steady stream of poems and essays. His collected works fill volumes. Lovecraft never made much money from his writing, but that didn't stop him. Lovecraft wrote like a man on a mission, like a man with a message he, and only he, could give to the world.

Uranus also played a huge role in Lovecraft's writing. He was more a Contrarian than a Trickster. He said no to science, industrialization, and the modern world in general. He also said no to the idea that mankind was advancing. As Lovecraft saw it, Western culture was in the midst of a slide into irredeemable decadence. He expressed these opinions directly in his criticism and essays, but they were most elegantly stated in his stories. There are no heroes in Lovecraft's tales. The human protagonists are typically feckless, deluded, or simply overwhelmed, and the monsters always win.

While Mercury and Uranus seem to work together as guests in an almost seamless fashion, the Moon goes its own way. The Moon is strongly placed in

Lovecraft's chart in Libra in the First House. This might have been an indicator of great popularity if the Moon weren't conjunct standoffish Uranus. As it turned out, Lovecraft had a lot of friends despite his prickly personality, but popularity did not come to him until after he was dead. The Moon in Lovecraft's chart also describes the singular relationship he had with his mother. The only child of a widow, he was coddled and protected throughout his youth. Even when his mother was hospitalized and forced to leave him, Lovecraft's aunts picked up the slack and continued to treat him like a young prince. When Lovecraft married at the age of thirty-four, he may have looked for the same kind of treatment from his wife, but she left him after just a few months.

However, the primary contribution of the archetypical Child was how it brought an awareness of Lovecraft's own emotional vulnerability to the forefront of his personality. This made him afraid, and, being a Leo by Sun sign, this childish fearfulness was something Lovecraft could not accept. So he went on the offensive. He made people who were already much more vulnerable than himself his enemy, and he attacked them over and over in his writings. Lovecraft's racism was personal. It wasn't based on doctrine or politics, and it extended to everyone who was different from himself and his white Anglo-Saxon forebearers. It was the misguided and defensive elitism of a man afraid of his own human vulnerability.

Obviously, the vulnerability and emotional sensitivity of the Moon also informed Lovecraft's fiction. This is one reason his tales are still read and enjoyed. However, by weaving his racist opinions into his message and publicly saying no to a large portion of humanity, Lovecraft's legacy has forever been tainted. He let his subjective feeling of vulnerability and fear cloud his mind and limit his message. At the same time, Lovecraft's bigotry reduced the noble Contrarian in his nature into the kind of insufferable crackpot that is best ignored.

Combinations

It would be impossible to discuss every possible combination of all the archetypical figures listed in this book. As I said, it is common for people to have three or more of these aspects in their horoscopes. Sometimes the archetypes that come into a person's life complement one another and sometimes they conflict, and the influence they have is always dependent on the personality described by the rest of the horoscope. Obviously, the situation can become quite complex.

In order to help you make some sense of this, there is a list in part 3 in which all the possible pairings of two of the individual archetypes are described. Keep in mind that the same oft-repeated disclaimer applies with these combinations. Every judgment we make about these archetypical figures interacting has to be made within the context of the personality described by the entire horoscope.

CHAPTER 15

No Aspects to
the Nodes

Just as there are plenty of horoscopes in which there are multiple aspects to the Nodes of the Moon, there are also some that (using the orbs described in chapter 13) have no aspects to the Nodes. Celebrity examples of this are not as easy to find, but they do exist. Here is an abbreviated list: Ben Affleck, Pamela Anderson, John Belushi, Yogi Berra, Camilla Duchess of Cornwall, Coco Chanel, Charles Dickens, Chris Evert, Rock Hudson, Charles Lindbergh, Bette Midler, Sean Penn, Meryl Streep, Barbara Walters, and George Washington.

There is, of course, one simple way of alleviating this situation. We can simply expand the orbs. As I've said, some astrologers use orbs for aspects that are much wider than the ones I've allowed for in this project. There is no hard-and-fast rule on this. The reason I set up the orbs for aspects to the Lunar Nodes the way I did is because I wanted to focus on only the strongest of those aspects. It is not unreasonable to assume that, in the absence of any close aspects to the Nodes, wider (and assumedly weaker) aspects might have more influence.

For an example of how this could work, we can look at the horoscope of President John F. Kennedy.

The North Node in Kennedy's chart is at 12 degrees and 29 minutes of Cancer. There are no aspects to the Nodes using the orbs I've set. The closest connection is a trine to the North Node from the Moon. It is separated by 4 degrees and 44 minutes. That's more than a full degree over the 3½-degree orb I've allowed. However, we can certainly see evidence of both the Adorable Child and the Misbehaving Child in John Kennedy's life.

John Kennedy's father wanted his Irish Catholic sons to fit into the dominant WASP culture, so he sent them to elite colleges where they were supposed to excel and impress, both in the classroom and on the playing fields. John's older brother, Joe Jr., did just that, but John was a sickly boy, and he spent much of his first year of college confined to his bed. However, by means of his Gemini wit and charm, John Kennedy was able to overcome this deficit, and by the end of his college career, he was the most popular young man on campus. We could certainly see this as the Moon aspecting the Nodes turning apparent vulnerability into phenomenal popularity.

Kennedy's health concerns continued after he left college, and they were compounded by an injury he suffered during World War II. His popularity also remained a strong factor, particularly with women. Despite the fact that he was often in pain, Kennedy's reputation as a womanizer increased at a pace equal to his standing as an ambitious politician. The fact that John Kennedy was charming, good-looking, and came from a wealthy family had something to do with this. So did the abysmal example that had been set by his philandering father. However, it is also possible that Kennedy's compulsive promiscuity stemmed from the lack of impulse control that we often see with the Moon aspecting the Nodes.

Considering these facts, an argument could be made for expanding the orb for the trine to the North Node to 5 degrees, at least in this chart. In Kennedy's horoscope, that would be easy to do, because it wouldn't create any other aspects. It might, however, make it tempting to push that orb out to 6 degrees so you could include Mars, which is separated from a trine to the North Node by 5 degrees and 57 minutes. After all, John Kennedy was a war hero. But was that evidence of Mars aspecting the Nodes, or was it the product of attributes already described in his horoscope? This is the sort of question that arises when you begin to push out the orbs of these aspects.

It is a slope that gets more slippery with each incremental increase of the orb. Pretty soon you have a situation in which no horoscope is without a half dozen or more aspects to the Nodes of the Moon. That might seem like a good thing, more grist for the mill, but I'm not so sure. Modern astrology offers us so many ways in which we can parse, prod, and squeeze information out of a horoscope that the most salient problem facing any astrologer may be knowing when to stop. Too much information can be just as limiting as too little. This is as true for aspects to the Nodes as it is for everything else about astrology.

Every indicator in a horoscope is elastic. That is to say, its essential meaning can be stretched in different directions. The role that the Hero or the Trickster plays in your life can vary greatly depending on how that archetype interacts with everything else in your horoscope. The more of these archetypes that you introduce into this interaction, the more complex it becomes. Regardless of how you approach them, the Lunar Nodes are an important part of the horoscope, and the aspects made to them give astrologers a powerful tool that can expand their knowledge. However, as with any powerful tool, it is important that we use the Nodes in a sensible and judicious manner.

There is another way of looking at these charts that don't have aspects to the Nodes using the orbs described here. That is to categorically say that there are no aspects to the Nodes. Some people might even want to make the orbs for these aspects tighter or throw out the quincunx, which is not among the traditional aspects. I don't necessarily recommend this, but there are some horoscopes in which saying no to the aspects to the Nodes seems to be the only appropriate approach.

We might wonder what it means when a person is born without aspects to the Nodes of the Moon. Have they somehow been left out of the great cosmic scheme? Are their horoscopes missing an important piece that everyone else seems to have? From the point of view of reincarnation, are they first timers, souls with no previous incarnations, or have they somehow been cut off from their past lives? Of course, we could also say that people born without any aspects to the Nodes of the Moon are people who are, for whatever reason, fully focused on *this* lifetime and that their spiritual reality is not subject to visitations from the past or the beyond. As we have seen, these aspects can create havoc in a person's life. Maybe the people with no aspects to the Nodes of the Moon are actually the lucky ones.

In the end, it is all a matter of what you need to make sense of the horoscope. Within the world of astrology, for every minimalist curmudgeon who growls about sticking to the basics, there is someone else who gleefully gathers exotic techniques and trans-Neptunian objects like they are Easter eggs. There's really no fault on either side. If you have a horoscope in which there are no aspects to the Nodes, or just too few to satisfy your tastes, what needs to be done is totally up to you.

CHAPTER 16

The Lunar Nodes on the Angles, Houses, and Signs

Astrologers refer to the Ascendant, Descendant, MC (midheaven or medium coeli), and IC (imum coeli) as the angles of the horoscope. They also represent (in most systems) the cusps of the First, Fourth, Seventh, and Tenth Houses. The angles are generally considered to be power points in the horoscope, and having a planet placed near one of them raises the importance of that archetype. Shouldn't it be the same with the Nodes of the Moon?

The problem is that the Nodes are not archetypes. Neither are the angles. The angles of the horoscope represent the basic functions within the personality that are associated with the houses they rule. The Ascendant is the self and how we want the world to see us. The IC is home and the influences of our family. The Descendant is marriage or partnership and the basic "other." And the MC, or midheaven, is career and the judgment of our peers. These functions don't come to us from some other place. They are each a basic part of being human. We really can't look at the connection between the Lunar Nodes and the angles in the same way that we look at aspects made by the planets.

Among my celebrity examples, as well as in the charts of friends, family, and clients, I have seen plenty of instances in which the Nodes of the Moon were conjunct either the Ascendant/Descendant axis or the MC/IC axis. However, I was never able find a theme or attribute that unified these people. Of course, I didn't have the archetypes to guide me in this search. One option is to consider these conjunctions (or squares, trines, or quincunxes) to put extra emphasis on the angle in question. In this theory, having the North Node on the midheaven would result in a person exhibiting extraordinary ambition and concern for their career. This is something that is difficult to discern with celebrity examples, since they tend to be ambitious people in general. However, when I look at my noncelebrity examples with the Nodes conjunct the midheaven, I do not see a consistent tendency in this direction.

This leads us to the function of the astrological houses. For a conjunction of the North Node to the midheaven, this would actually be the Tenth House/Fourth House axis, since when the North Node conjuncts the MC, the South Nodes will naturally conjunct the IC. The same reasoning applies to a conjunction by the North Node to the Ascendant and the First and Seventh Houses.

Houses

Any discussion of the Nodes of the Moon and the astrological houses has to begin with the notion of the Nodes as a gateway to a higher or broader spiritual reality. The house placement of the Lunar Nodes describes the way in which our spiritual essence is translated into the mundane operations of real life. The conjunction of the Nodes of the Moon with the angles might indicate that extra emphasis is or should be placed on this process, but since it is happening at such a deep, spiritual level, that is a distinction that can only be made by that person and (possibly) by an advisor who has intimate knowledge of that person's spiritual life.

In discussing the placement of the Nodes of the Moon in the houses, we must first recognize that they are not like aspects. As we have seen, when it comes to aspects to the Nodes, there is no difference between the North or the South Node (except in the case of aspects from the Sun). However, that doesn't necessarily mean that the dichotomy between North and South Nodes is not effective when applied to other astrological factors, such as house placements. For one thing, the houses are themselves dichotomous. The First House, which is about self, is opposite the Seventh, which is about others. The Tenth House, which represents career and public life, is opposite the Fourth, which represents home and family. In the context of the astrological houses, seeing the North and South Nodes as opposites seems completely appropriate.

Looking at the Nodes of the Moon in this way sets up an interesting dynamic. The basic idea is that the house that contains the South Nodes shows you the area of life that dominated your past life, as well as the habits and skills that you bring into this life from the past. These are things that might seem natural to you, but they will not aid your spiritual development. The house containing your North Node, on the other hand, represents a new direction that you must take if you wish to continue your spiritual growth.

Without archetypical images to sort of jazz them up, the meaning of the Nodes in the houses might seem rather prosaic. We have no Stars, Tricksters, or Dreamers here. We are simply talking about different areas of life, the basic operations of knowing yourself, feeding yourself, and deciding whom you want to be with. Even the more exciting houses still have a substantial connection to the dull routine of living. In order to support the higher mind of the Ninth House, you have to go to school. In order to enjoy the comradery of the Eleventh House of intentional community, you have to get dressed and go to meetings. The Nodes of the Moon are still our gateway to the great mystery of the universe, but, with the houses, that mystery is actualized within the context of the unremarkable workings of the real world.

The dichotomous placement of the Lunar Nodes in the houses calls upon you to change. It calls for you to move away from the comfort and stagnation of the house holding the South Node toward the discomfort and growth demanded by the house occupied by the North Node. This movement is by no means an easy thing to do. It requires a long-term struggle and backsliding is common. It is also subtle. It is subtle because, just like the aspects to the Lunar Nodes, their house placement functions on a different level than the personality described by the rest of the horoscope. Even though the influence of the Nodes is actualized through the everyday processes of living, that influence is primarily spiritual. Many people might not even be aware of how they are being pulled from one area of life and toward another. Depending on their sensitivity to such issues, they might have trouble recognizing this movement even when it is pointed out to them.

In part 3, you will find a list describing how the North and South Nodes function in each of the twelve houses.

Signs

Some astrologers like to equate the signs of the zodiac with the astrological houses. This is particularly the case when they are discussing the dichotomy of the North and South Nodes of the Moon. They might indicate that the South Node in Aries means the same thing as the South Node in the First House. There is a strong connection between Aries and the meaning of the First House, just as there is a connection between Taurus and the Second, Gemini and the Third, and so on. However, that connection does not mean that Aries and the First House are the same or function in the same way.

We can see this more clearly if we break it down in theatrical terms. The planet is the actor, and the sign is the role the actor plays. Different actors will play the same roles in different ways. Sir Ian McKellen's King Lear would not be the same as Sir Patrick Stewart's King Lear. Likewise, the way Mars plays the role of Aries is quite different from the way Venus or Mercury would play that role.

The house occupied by the planet represents the setting in which this role is acted out. That setting is going to dictate some of what the actor says and does just as much as the role they are playing, but they are going to do this in very different ways. The role is not the setting, and the setting is not the role.

Of course, the Lunar Nodes are not planets, and, as we have seen, the way they behave in a particular setting (or house) is more subtle and spiritual. We have to assume that the same would apply to the way the Nodes take on a role (or sign).

In part 3, you will find a list of how the North and South Nodes function in each of the twelve signs.

CHAPTER 17

Transits Involving the Lunar Nodes

Transiting aspects reveal the true magic of astrology. Character analysis is fine, but there is a directness and simplicity to the way transits work that is often mind-blowing. A faraway planet moving along the ecliptic aligns with a significant point in your natal horoscope, and *bang*, something happens. There is no physical reason why something should happen, and yet it happens again and again. It doesn't even have to be a dramatic event. You're wide-awake at 3:00 a.m. You check your ephemeris and see that the Moon is passing over your Mars. You spend an hour searching your house for your car keys only to find them still in the ignition of your car. What's going on? Transiting Mercury was square your Neptune.

In these moments, we truly feel the connection between our earthly selves and the greater universe, and, even in the most unhappy of times, feeling that connection can be a comfort. Looking at things from a broader perspective, we can see how longer transits like the cyclic aspects of Saturn and the contacts involving the slower-moving outer planets create the underlying structure of our lives. We feel the pull of these aspects. We negotiate the hazards they present us and try to take advantage of the opportunities they bring. But, most of all, we learn what they have to teach us.

One thing I do for fun is read biographies and note the dates of important events in the subject's life. Then I look at how transiting aspects to that person's horoscope align with those events. I've been doing this for many years, and I've studied several hundred biographies in this way. This process has given me a healthy respect for the efficacy of certain transiting aspects. Saturn cycle aspects, both angular aspects (squares, oppositions, and conjunctions) to the planet's natal place and conjunctions to the four angles (Ascendant, IC, Descendant, and MC), rarely occur without some corresponding event. Angular aspects by Uranus to the Sun and Moon and its conjunctions to the four angles are also in my top tier of indicators. Angular aspects by Neptune and Pluto to the Sun and Moon and their conjunctions to the angles can also be powerful, though their influence tends to be more subtle and drawn out over a longer period.

Other transits, such as aspects by the outer planets to Mercury, Venus, and Mars in the natal chart can also be important, but their influence tends to be specific to the planets involved. The influence of trines, sextiles, and quincunxes by these outer planets is not generally as dramatic or reliable in terms of their connection to actual events. This might be because their influence is more likely to support continuity than bring changes.

This long study of transiting aspects has taught me something about the transits of the Lunar Nodes. Compared to the transits of Saturn, Uranus, and so forth, they do not seem to be reliable indicators of change, at least not in the context of observable events in a person's public life. There are striking exceptions to this trend, but they are not consistent. Transiting Mars squaring the Nodes in your natal horoscope might be significant in one instance and then pass unnoticed in another.

I've heard plenty of anecdotal testimony from other people as to the effectiveness of transits of the Nodes of the Moon. However, these testimonies generally don't mention other transits that might have contributed to the event in question. Also, depending on the orbs you are using, if we are considering both transiting aspects that the Lunar Nodes are making to planets in your natal chart and the ones being made by transiting planets to the Nodes of the Moon, it is a rare day that doesn't feature some nodal transit.

The problem is determining which of these aspects has special significance, and there is no consensus on that issue.

Mundane Astrology

How these transits work in natal astrology is one thing, but we also need to consider the way they function on mundane astrology. Mundane astrology is the study of astrology of historical events. We can often learn something about what transiting aspects mean to us on a personal level by observing what is happening in the world when these aspects are in force. What follows is a selection of events in which hard aspects to the Nodes seem to be a factor.

- September 1, 1939 (Germany invaded Poland, starting World War II): Transiting Saturn conjunct the transiting South Node of the Moon with Pluto square both.
- May 14, 1948 (First Arab-Israeli War): Transiting Pluto square the Lunar Nodes.
- October 6, 1973 (Yom Kippur War): Transiting Pluto square the Lunar Nodes.
- September 11, 2001 (Terrorist attacks on the World Trade Center and the Pentagon): Transiting Mars conjunct the transiting South Node and opposing the Moon, which was conjunct the North Node.
- July 14, 2014 (Passenger plane shot down over Ukraine): Transiting Mars conjunct the North Node with both conjunct the Ascendant and square the transiting Sun.
- November 13, 2015 (Terrorist attacks in Paris): Transiting Mars conjunct the transiting North Node with both on the IC.

This list of events does indicate that aspects to the Nodes can be a factor in dramatic, historical events. However, nothing in a horoscope happens in a vacuum. Other factors are always at play. For example, on September 1, 1939, Saturn was square Pluto. On October 6, 1973, Saturn was square Pluto again. On September 11, 2001, Saturn was opposed to Pluto. The connection between angular aspects involving Saturn and Pluto with war and increased international tension is well established, so we might say that those aspects were the primary indicators in these instances. We also have to consider the event in historical context. The first Arab-Israeli War was a reaction to the establishment of the state of Israel, which had been mandated by the United Nations in September 1947, when Saturn was conjunct Pluto.

One reason that transiting aspects to the Lunar Nodes seem elusive may have to do with what they represent in the horoscope. When relating historical events to the movement of the planets, astrologers look at the symbolism associated with the planets involved. It follows that when the finality and lack of compassion that are part of the archetype of Saturn clash with the need for power and extremism that is part of the archetype of Pluto, you just might end up with a war. However, as we have seen, the Nodes of the Moon are not archetypes. They are gateways through which the archetypes may come into our lives. They are also our gateway to the mystery of fate and the unstoppable force of destiny.

The "Mystery"

Just as aspects involving the Lunar Nodes in the natal chart represent factors that are separate from the basic structure of the personality, transiting aspects to and by the Nodes function in very different ways than transiting aspects to and by the planets. Instead of representing the interaction of two archetypes, these nodal transits bring us a message. What you consider to be the source of that message depends on you and your religious and spiritual background. For the purposes of this discussion, let's just label it the "mystery."

These messages from the mystery are by no means rare. Transiting aspects involving the Nodes of the Moon occur constantly throughout our lifetimes, and, with each of these aspects, we might assume that we are getting a message. How receptive we are to that message will depend on many factors, such as our degree of spiritual awareness and how prepared we are, psychologically, to deal with the content of that particular message. Generally speaking, it would seem that a lot of people a lot of the time are not attuned to these messages. For this reason, these transits seem to come and go without any discernable change in the physical, intellectual, or (as much as we can tell) spiritual circumstances of our lives.

This brings us back to the bias that is built into using a database of famous people. Most of the people who become the subjects of biographies (or articles and interviews) are not especially spiritual. Even when they are, a person's spiritual development tends to be personal and subjective. Tying it to specific dates is often difficult. There are, of course, exceptions. In chapter 10, we met Bernadette Soubirous, the girl who saw a vision of the Virgin Mary while gathering firewood in the forest. On February 11, 1858, when Bernadette had her vison, transiting Neptune was within 1 degree of a square to her natal Nodes of the Moon. Obviously, the message to Bernadette from a Visionary archetype of Neptune was delivered in an emphatic, easily discernable fashion. However, these moments when spiritual transcendence intersects real-life events are relatively rare.

Fortunately, even those of us who are not particularly spiritually aware have a spiritual life. We may not acknowledge it or keep track of its progress, but it is always there. For this reason, events that might seem to have relevance only to our life in the "real" world can also significantly impact us in a spiritual way. These events are not always, or even often, the "big" events of our life. They are not the events that mark our professional and social advancement. Those events typically have more to do with the transits of Saturn, Uranus, and the other outer planets (along with secondary progressions and other factors). Events that can be linked to aspects involving the Nodes of the Moon are often events in which fate seems to make a random entry into our lives. For example, in 1912, the American author Theodore Dreiser had booked passage from Europe to the United States on the maiden voyage of the Titanic. At the last moment, contrary to his typically free-spending lifestyle, Dreiser decided to switch to a cheaper option. We all know how the maiden voyage of the Titanic ended. That switch saved the author's life, and Dreiser made this fateful decision when the transiting Nodes were square his natal Neptune and Jupiter.

Not all these encounters with the mystery of fate are so fortunate for the person involved. Serial killer Jeffrey Dahmer was captured and the teenage Eva Braun met the love of her life (Adolf Hitler) when the transiting North

Node was conjunct Saturn in their respective charts. In both cases, there were other important transits going on at the time of the event. However, it is by no means a stretch to say that, along with the way these events changed the physical situation of each of these people, they also had special relevance to their spiritual existence.

In part 3, you will find a list of nodal transits to the natal horoscope. These summaries are based on information drawn from the lives of my celebrity examples. For each combination, I looked at both aspects by the transiting Nodes of the Moon to planets and other sensitive points in the natal horoscope and aspects by transiting planets to the natal Nodes of the Moon. For the purpose of this project, I considered only angular aspects (conjunctions and squares) with an orb of no more than 2 degrees. This doesn't mean that I dismiss the notion that other aspects might be important. Once again, I wanted to focus just on those contacts I felt would be the most dynamic and reliable.

PART
THREE

I've read enough astrology books to know that no one reads a book on this subject in the same way they read a novel. We don't begin at page 1 and keep turning pages until we get to the end. Instead, we go to the sections that interest us most, which are typically the pages that are about us, and read them first. Then we might move on to the pages that relate to our family or friends. If we like what we see, we might flip back to page 1 and proceed.

This section of the book is designed to help you with that process, particularly with the house and sign placements of the Lunar Nodes and with transiting aspects involving the Nodes. You should keep in mind, though, that the summaries provided here are general and abbreviated. A complete understanding of any of these factors would require a much more in-depth study. It would also require knowledge of your circumstances and, of course, your complete horoscope. These summaries are designed to be appetizers. The actual meal starts on page 1.

CHAPTER 18

Matching the Archetype with the Chart

T hroughout this book, I've talked about how the personality and character described by the horoscope as a whole can either subdue or exagger-
ate the archetypical figures brought into our lives by aspects to the Nodes of
the Moon. What follows is a list of each of these archetypes and the condi-
tions in the horoscope that can either help or hinder that archetype extend its
influence into your life.

The Sun (The Star, Hero, and Leader)

Among the things that might strengthen this guest, particularly when it's
aspecting the North Node, is an emphasis on signs that are prone to expansive, egotistic behaviors, such as Leo, Aries, and, to a lesser degree, Sagittarius. Also, strong aspects (including squares and oppositions) by Jupiter to the
Sun or Moon and the placement of the Sun in the First or Tenth House tend
to provide a solid footing for the prideful tendencies of the Sun aspecting the
North Node.

Among the components of a horoscope that would discourage the Sun
from aspecting the North Node are having the Sun placed in signs like Pisces

or Virgo that tend to less comfortable in the spotlight, the placement of the Sun in the Sixth or Twelfth House, or strong aspects to the Sun (excluding trines and sextiles) by Saturn, Neptune, or Pluto. Having Mars in some way debilitated in the chart might also cause this archetype to stumble, and the placement of Saturn, Neptune, or Pluto on the angles of the chart (Ascendant, midheaven, Descendant, and IC) can provide significant impediments to the expansion of the ego.

With the Sun aspecting the South Node of the Moon, the situation is different. Though factors that have an expansive influence on the ego can be helpful, what you really have to be aware of are the character flaws described in the chart. Every horoscope contains at least the possibility of some significant weakness or another. That is a given. With the Sun aspecting the South Node, the possibility of those private failings being broadcast to the public and leading to failure or disgrace greatly increases. Understanding the nature of these flaws and minimalizing their influence can improve the manner in which you coexist with the Sun aspecting the South Node.

The Moon (The Child)

The Moon aspecting the Nodes presents us with a special problem. Though the archetype is always the Child, there are several ways in which that Child can come forth. There is the Adorable Child, the Vulnerable Child, the child who can't control their impulses, and the child whose innocence and instinctive goodness are an inspiration to us all. The personality described by the horoscope will certainly help determine which face of the archetype will predominate, but the situation is different for each face.

The Adorable Child is typically helped by some of the same factors that augment the ego when the Sun is conjunct the North Node of the Moon, such as a strong placement of the Sun or Jupiter. The placement of the Moon is also important. Having the Moon in the First or Tenth House is, by itself, an indicator of popularity, and that popularity becomes even more likely when it is teamed with the Moon aspecting the Nodes.

Even though the examples we have of the Good Child are few, aspects involving Neptune and strong placement in the Twelfth House, both of which can indicate self-sacrifice, seem to stand out.

Of course, those are the faces of this archetype we want to encourage. The Misbehaving Child and the Vulnerable Child, on the other hand, are faces we would prefer to avoid. With the Misbehaving Child, you have to be aware of Mars and Uranus. If either planet is prominent in the chart, impulse control can be difficult. Self-indulgence is typically helped along by aspects to the personal planets by Neptune or Jupiter.

The Vulnerable Child presents us with a more complex situation. Primarily, we would look for placements and aspects that might weaken the ego or produce a malleable or impressionable personality. These might include debilitating aspects to the Sun by Saturn or Neptune, a predominance of mutable signs, or an emphasis on the Twelfth House in the horoscope.

Another issue that can have relevance to both the Misbehaving Child and the Vulnerable Child is a predominance of signs that have trouble revealing their vulnerability, such as Scorpio, Capricorn, and Leo. People with these aspects who deny their vulnerability might be inclined to compensate for it by acting tougher than they are and by misbehaving.

Mercury (The Messenger)

The Messenger requires a clear and outwardly directed mind. A mind that is hobbled by insecurity and fear or clouded by greed, lust, or addiction will not provide the kind of basis from which this archetype can work. The potential for these impediments can certainly be seen in the horoscope, but to a large extent, they are also a product of decisions and choices made by the individual.

As for indicators in the chart that can facilitate the Messenger, the most obvious is having the Sun placed in the Ninth House. Having other bodies in the Ninth strongly aspected can also be a positive factor. Similar situations involving the Third House can also help, though the message will likely be more localized. Having Mercury strongly placed in the chart would also tend to augment this archetype, as would having that planet in Mercury-ruled signs (Gemini and Virgo) or air signs (Gemini, Libra, and Aquarius).

Venus (The Feminine)

Venus represents the Divine Feminine within us all, and our ability to get the most out of this archetype is often dependent on how we relate to the women in our lives. Factors in the chart that might hamper those relationships, like hard aspects to the Moon, can definitely make finding your way to that feminine power source more difficult, regardless of your gender. Squares and oppositions to Venus can also negatively influence the way you see women as individuals and the feminine inside yourself.

On the other hand, having Venus or the Moon strongly placed in the chart or in friendly signs (Taurus, Libra, and Pisces for Venus; Cancer or Taurus for the Moon) can ease your way to this archetype. Strong placements by the Sun and Mars are not necessarily negative. They can allow women with these aspects to bring feminine energy in areas generally considered masculine. However, you must be aware that the ego-driven needs of the Sun and Mars are not always compatible with the goals of the feminine.

Mars (The Warrior)

We explored how the personality described by different horoscopes can stifle or expand this archetype's role in chapter 13. Mars aspecting the Nodes needs a chart in which autonomy and initiative are supported by aspects to and the placement of both Mars and the Sun. It functions best with a Sun that is placed in a fire sign or a sign ruled by Mars (Aries or Scorpio). When the Sun is in less proactive signs, like Pisces, Virgo, or Libra, this archetypical visitor can struggle. This can also be the case when the Sun, Moon, or Mars are subject to restrictive aspects from Saturn or Pluto.

Jupiter (Faith)

When considering how Jupiter aspecting the Nodes will work within a horoscope, the first thing you must do is look at Neptune in that chart. People who have Neptune in a strong aspect with one of the personal planets, particularly the Sun or the Moon, are already predisposed to ignore boundaries and find satisfaction in the obliteration of the ego. For those who are inclined toward the religious side of this archetype, these tendencies may lead to a heightened spirituality, but it can also result in a dangerous surrender of objectivity. For the Libertine people in this group, it brings the possibility of substance abuse and addiction.

Otherwise, charts most conducive to bringing out the capacity for faith that we see with Jupiter aspecting the Nodes are those with a predominance of fire signs. These are people who are excited about their faith, whether it's faith in a religious creed, a political party, or the next roll of the dice. When air signs predominate in the horoscope, people tend to be less fervent and more intellectual in the way they approach these issues. Water sign people are apt to be committed True Believers, though their focus is often more on personal matters.

Earth sign people, on the other hand, are typically too practical to be carried away by either a belief system or hedonistic pleasures. Aspects by Saturn to the personal planets can have the same outcome: they make these people more susceptible to doubt. The same goes for people with Pluto emphasized by aspect or placement. These folks tend to question everything, and that makes faith difficult to sustain.

Saturn (Doubt)

Not surprisingly, the same factors that discourage faith can encourage doubt. Aspects by Saturn or Pluto to the personal planets make it easier for doubt to take root and spread. However, these are instances when people with these aspects do a better job of containing and channeling their self-doubt, because they have a deeper understanding of its influence on their personality.

In chapter 9, I compared golfers Jack Nicklaus and George Archer, both of whom had Saturn aspecting the Nodes. A detailed comparison of their horoscopes shows that both featured significant indicators of success and accomplishment. The main difference was the fact that Archer had Neptune prominently placed in his chart. Neptune's heightened presence allowed Archer to convince himself that he could hide his doubt by avoiding interviews and endorsement deals. He succeeded, but at the cost of his career. Nicklaus, who felt the same self-doubt but refused to let it hinder him, is still considered a major figure in the sports world. Archer, on the other hand, is largely forgotten.

Generally speaking, horoscopes in which Jupiter is active can help the people with these aspects avoid being paralyzed by self-doubt. Also, factors that augment the ego, such as a prominently placed Sun or strong placements in Leo, Aries, and Sagittarius, can make it easier for a person to feel the doubt and continue to perform at a high level.

Uranus

The big question when Uranus aspects the Lunar Nodes is whether you will be one of those people who creates mischief or one of those who is subject to mischief created for you by history or fate. To a certain extent, these two categories overlap. The Contrarians and Tricksters of the world often get themselves into dicey situations in which they are at risk of being carried away by the winds of change. After all, the basic purpose of the mischief brought out by this archetype is to upset sameness, certainty, and stability.

People with Uranus aspecting one of their personal planets, as well as the Nodes, tend to be more likely to embrace the role of the Trickster or the Contrarian, and, by doing this, they are often better able to ride out these waves of change. On the other hand, people with charts in which Uranus is isolated and not connected to the personal planets are more likely to be taken unawares by sudden changes. They're not in on the joke and tend to hold on to the status quo longer than they should.

Another factor is flexibility. People with these aspects who have a predominance of fixed signs in their charts or are weighed down by heavy aspects to Saturn or Pluto can also be at a disadvantage. They might be all for disrupting the status quo, but only for the purposes of replacing it with a different status quo more to their liking. This attitude has no place in the agenda of this archetype. No status quo, even one of your own creation, is immune to the Trickster's wiles.

Neptune

Assessing whether or not an aspect to the Nodes by Neptune will take root in a horoscope should, in theory, be simple. If the chart is laden with practical indicators (an emphasis on Earth signs or a prominently placed Saturn), then it will probably resist the Dreamer or the Visionary. Also, a chart with strong, intellectual, or rational indicators, such as a predominance of air signs or strong aspects involving the personal planets and Uranus, would seem an unlikely environment for the archetype.

On the other hand, a highly emotional chart with a lot of water signs or a strongly placed Moon would seem more conducive to Neptune's nonrational influence. Fire signs could also be helpful, as can aspects and placements of Mars and Jupiter that describe a susceptibility to inspiration or impulsive behavior. Pursuing your vision requires a leap of faith, and the ability to make such a leap sometimes has more to do with courage than emotion.

However, when you actually look at the horoscopes of the people who seem to get the best out of these aspects, what you often find is a balance of these factors. Saint Bernadette was a Capricorn by Sun sign. In her chart, that Capricorn practicality was offset by Mars in imaginative Pisces, but it was the combination of these two indicators that made Bernadette's testimony about her vision so convincing, both to the people in her village and to herself.

It's not enough just to have a Vision. You have to be able to articulate that Vision in a concrete and believable fashion. You also have to be able to locate ways in which you can at least attempt to apply your Vision to the real world. Visionaries who lack these capacities are unlikely to ever see their visons realized.

Pluto

We began this discussion with the Sun and questions about ego. With Pluto, appropriately enough, ego is once again the central issue. However, here the question is, Can you let go of ego? Can you surrender your will, your control, your power without anger or remorse, without feeling cheated or abused?

Answering yes to this question often depends on the propensies described in your horoscope. If the Sun is strongly placed in the chart and/or there are positive aspects to the personal planets by Mars or Jupiter, then dealing with Pluto's demands can pose a significant challenge. People with the Sun in a less advantageous position or who have other placements or aspects that subdue the ego typically have an easier time finding their way to transformation.

CHAPTER 19

Combinations

W hat follows is a list of all the possible pairings of two of the archetypes that come into our lives through aspects to the Nodes of the
Moon. The information provided here is only designed to give the reader a
hint as to the dynamic of each pairing. The basic character described by the
rest of the horoscope, as well as any other aspects to the Lunar Nodes, will
always play a major role in how any two archetypes interact.

Combinations with the Sun Aspecting the Nodes

The Sun with the Moon

This one changes depending on whether the Sun is aspecting the North Node
or the South Node. At first glance, the former seems to be a brilliant combination, putting together leadership with popularity. However, the emotional-
ism of the Moon does not always work well with the Sun's focus on the ego.
It can create a leader whose decisions are subjective and self-serving. It can
also create a leader who secretly feels vulnerable and views any criticism as a
threat to their emotional security.

If the Sun is aspecting the South Node and the Moon the North, the vulnerability of the Moon is often more pronounced and obvious. In some cases, people with this combination can turn that vulnerability into an asset. In others, it will become an impediment to the exercise of their solar ego.

The Sun with Mercury

This combination describes a Messenger who speaks with great confidence and style. Your message is also likely to be intertwined with your ego and pride. This won't necessarily make your message any less valid, but it will detract from its objectivity.

The Sun with Venus

The full expression of your solar ego will have a lot to do with how you relate to the feminine, both inside yourself and as it is represented by the women in your life. For some men, this could be a challenge. You might have to share the spotlight with a woman who played or plays a significant role in your life, and this could eat at your pride.

The Sun with Mars

For the Heroes with the Sun aspecting the Nodes, this would seem to be the perfect combination, combining phenomenal courage with a fighting spirit. But it could also create a situation in which the Warrior becomes such an intrinsic part of your ego that you don't know when to stop fighting. If you have the Sun aspecting the South Node, you might find yourself fighting for a lost cause.

The Sun with Jupiter

When the Sun is aspecting the North Node, this combination has the potential of producing a spiritual or political Leader or Hero. The same could also apply when the Sun is conjunct the South Node, only your leadership might not be quite so celebrated. In both instances, the Libertine with this combination is likely to have difficulty balancing self-indulgence with dignity.

The Sun with Saturn

For those of you with the Sun aspecting the North Node, this could be a positive combination. It is a wise Leader whose leadership is informed by a modicum of doubt. On the other hand, the egotism of the Sun could make it difficult for you to submit to the Teacher's authority. This is particularly likely if you have the Sun aspecting the South Node.

The Sun with Uranus

You can't be a good Contrarian or Trickster unless you also have courage and self-confidence. That makes this a generally positive combination regardless of which Node is being aspected by the Sun. However, you have to be aware that too much ego can make the Contrarian seem selfish and the Trickster seem cruel.

The Sun with Neptune

This might seem to be an undesirable combination, but each of these archetypes gives the other what it most needs. The Sun can give the Visionary within you the courage and self-confidence to pursue your vision, regardless of whatever opposition you might face, while Neptune gives the Star, the Leader, and the Hero a purpose beyond mere egotism.

The Sun with Pluto

Pluto often demands that we surrender our will and our ego to a power greater than ourselves. For people with the Sun aspecting the North Node, this can seem like an impossible task. People with the Sun aspecting the South Node might have an easier time, but much depends on how well they've learned the lessons of that placement.

Combinations with the Moon Aspecting the Nodes

The Moon with Mercury

Say what you feel. This is something that comes easily to people with this combination. Here, the Messenger speaks with the emotional power and seductive charm of the Moon. It is a message spoken in a soft voice that is, nonetheless, nearly impossible to resist.

The Moon with Venus

Having a strong-willed woman in your life could be necessary for your emotional security. However, women with this combination may struggle to balance a sense of their emotional vulnerability with the need to display the strength of the feminine. One might seem to cancel out the other. Men with this combination might seem exceptionally attractive to women.

The Moon with Mars

Your battles are always personal. In many instances, this will make you a more determined and ruthless fighter. However, no matter how tough you may think you are, you go into every battle with your heart wide open. You will be hurt, and how you deal with that pain and what you learn from those wounds will be what really determines who wins the fight.

The Moon with Jupiter

The capacity for self-indulgence that we sometimes see with the Moon aspecting the Nodes blends all too well with the Libertine's brand of faith. The result could be a dangerous lack of self-control. However, the True Believers with this combination will have the capacity of expressing their beliefs in a way that is both meaningful and deeply personal.

The Moon with Saturn

In some cases, this combination seems to work better than we might expect. The Child submits to the lessons of the Teacher and profits from them. However, as we saw with Marilyn Monroe, there are other times when Saturn's doubt tends to feed the fearfulness of the Moon. Instead of instructing, the Teacher intimidates and sets standards you feel you cannot meet.

The Moon with Uranus

Neither the Contrarian nor the Trickster are well served by an excess of emotional sensitivity. Mischief-making generally requires a thick skin. On the other hand, the innocence of the Child will always make it easier for you to find forgiveness, no matter how disruptive and rebellious your actions might be.

The Moon with Neptune

You have an emotional commitment to your Vision, and that gives that Vision extra power. However, with this combination there is also the possibility that your Vision will become too personal, subjective, and infected with fear and insecurity. This is a tendency of which you must always be wary.

The Moon with Pluto

The emotional openness of the Moon can actually make it easier for you to accept the fundamental changes brought about by Pluto. You are not afraid to surrender your ego and open yourself to new possibilities. This is particularly true with the slow, incremental transformations that Pluto sometimes brings us. Your emotionality can give you a deeper understanding of the importance of these processes.

Combinations with Mercury Aspecting the Nodes

Mercury with Venus

The message you bring to the world has been informed either by the influence of a woman in your life or by your awareness of the Divine Feminine within yourself. This might not make your message clearer or more urgent, but it will increase the pleasure you get from seeing it delivered.

Mercury with Mars

There is an edge to your message that might make it seem more like a challenge than simple information. Whether or not it is your intention, some people might find this offensive and respond accordingly. At the same time, even though you are not necessarily looking for an argument, anyone who thinks they can just shut you up is in for a fight.

Mercury with Jupiter

You need to be able to share your faith, and the way you interject that belief and hope into your message can be truly inspirational. On the other hand, this same need to spread the word can work against you on a social level. The fact that some people don't want to hear your message may occur to you, but, in all probability, not nearly often enough.

Mercury with Saturn

The Teacher speaks through you, and this can give your message an authority that is reassuring to some people and intimidating to others. At the same time, there is often a subtext of doubt in your message. It's not that you doubt the ultimate truth of what you are saying; it's more that you doubt the ability of the world to understand that truth and do something positive with it.

Mercury with Uranus

The Messenger and the Trickster are natural allies. The Messenger understands the value of a little mischief when it comes to getting people's attention, and communication is a key element of every Trickster's art.

Mercury with Neptune

You are a Messenger who has been inspired by a Vision. However, delivering that message in a clear, rational way can be a challenge for you. What Neptune shows us can be amorphous, vague, and hard to describe. The Messenger who doesn't have the right training or the right tools to bring clarity out of this vagueness is bound to have a difficult time.

Mercury with Pluto

The message you bring to the world is so deep and so profound that you don't really expect people to understand it. This could cause you to consider remaining quiet. However, there is always going to be a part of you that longs for people to see things as you do. So, even though you know it's hopeless, you continue to deliver your message and to hone and improve it. It is out of this constant effort, this need to be understood, that your transformation will most likely come.

Combinations with Venus Aspecting the Nodes

Venus with Mars

Your relationships with the women in your life are apt to be competitive. This is true for both men and women. This combination could also represent a situation in which you have to fight or otherwise use masculine aggression in order to assert the power of the feminine that resides within your soul.

Venus with Jupiter

Your relationship either with an important woman in your life or with your own femininity (depending on your gender or sexual orientation) could take on the attributes of a cause or political statement. Another possibility is that religion or a belief system could figure prominently in these matters.

Venus with Saturn

With this combination, you have to be careful not to let your self-doubts infect your feelings toward the women in your life. These doubts can also cause you to see the feminine in your own nature as a weakness rather than a strength.

Venus with Uranus

You likely feel yourself drawn to women who display the qualities of either the Contrarian or the Trickster. This might be because you are drawn to the uniqueness of such people or because these women help you recognize and access your own Uranian tendencies.

Venus with Neptune

There is something Visionary and larger than life about your conception of the feminine. You search for a woman—as a lover, as a mentor, or just as a friend—who can live up to this Vision. Establishing a compromise between your Vision and the realities of human nature could become a major theme in your life.

Venus with Pluto

Pluto aspecting the Nodes brings us transformation, and this combination tells us that either a woman or your conception of the feminine will play a significant role in that transformation.

Combinations with Mars Aspecting the Nodes

Mars with Jupiter

You are not just a True Believer, you are a Warrior. You will fight for what you believe. This can be a positive combination, particularly when the beliefs you are fighting for are productive and truthful. However, you must beware a tendency to see belief systems other than your own as competitors and your interactions with them as a battle. This will only distract you from the good work of which you are so capable.

Mars with Saturn

If you're a fighter, you have to get used to taking it on the chin once in a while. Fighters lose as well as win. For those of you who can accept this fact, doubt poses no problem. For those of you who cannot, doubt will detract from your effectiveness as a Warrior and, in some cases, cause you to run away from the really big fights.

Mars with Uranus

You are an inventive Warrior who finds unique ways of winning. Going toe-to-toe with an opponent is really not your style. Some might accuse you of trickery and of refusing to obey the traditional rules of engagement. To them you say, "So what?"

Mars with Neptune

You are typically not as inclined to openly confront your enemies as most people with Mars aspecting the Nodes. You understand that your Vision is too delicate, too dependent on emotionality and the nonrational to endure the sharp give-and-take of debate. So, you hold back, and you wait, confident that the ultimate realization of your Vision (which you know is coming soon) will sweep your detractors from the field.

Mars with Pluto

You may come on a little too strong at times. This is because you are a Warrior who doesn't just expect to win the contest; you expect that your victory will result in nothing short of a transformation, both for you and for those who dared to oppose you.

Combinations with Jupiter Aspecting the Nodes

Jupiter with Saturn

You spend your life trying to balance opposites—optimism against pessimism, too much against too little, faith against doubt. Most of the time this balancing act keeps you pretty close to the middle of the road. However, if that balance ever tilts too far to one side or the other, getting back to the middle ground can be very difficult.

Jupiter with Uranus

You have boundless faith in your ability to get away with every trick and say no to every convention. This can make you a unique individual. It can also make you a fun and remarkably attractive companion. However, you need to be prepared for that day when your luck decides to take a vacation and all your tricks and defiance come back to haunt you.

Jupiter with Neptune

There is nothing more powerful in the long term than the combination of faith and Vision. In the short term, however, it can make you appear odd and unworldly. Your judgments might not always seem fair or realistic, and some people may regard you as weak or unreliable. When your Vision is realized and your faith justified, of course, none of that will matter.

Jupiter with Pluto

For you, faith is a means to power, to certainty, and to transformation. You don't care too much about rules made by other people or society. You may obey them just to be polite, but your faith is much too important, much too profound, to be confined by earthly concerns.

Combinations with Saturn Aspecting the Nodes

Saturn with Uranus

Doubt is not usually conducive to the activity of either the Contrarian or the Trickster. On the other hand, this combination could indicate that the lessons of the Teacher may come to you in unusual and disruptive ways.

Saturn with Neptune

In some cases, with this combination, your Vision becomes your Teacher. In others, your focus on your Vision makes it difficult for you to absorb what the Teacher is trying to teach you.

Saturn with Pluto

It is not impossible for a person to be transformed by doubt, but it can only happen after a journey through the darkness that requires both great courage and no small amount of desperation.

Combinations with Uranus Aspecting the Nodes

Uranus with Neptune

The vision that captivates your heart and soul is likely to take you to some strange and unexpected places. You may not always seem on track, and there may be times when forces beyond your control seem to take over. But, if your vision is true and untainted by ego or negativity, this wild ride could end with you sitting atop the mountain, looking down on a crazy dream that somehow came true.

Uranus with Pluto

Your mischief has a way of getting out of control and doing things you never intended for it to do. Sometimes this works in your favor, and other times the little joke you were playing on the world backfires, and you find yourself in the midst of a transformation you never expected.

Combinations with Neptune Aspecting the Nodes

Neptune with Pluto

Your visions should not be taken lightly, by you or anyone else, because they can have far-reaching ramifications. You see a way not just to change, but to transform, both for yourself and for the world in which you live. Most of you will never realize the full power that comes with this kind of Vision, but even those of you who just strive in that direction are likely to be regarded by your peers with a certain degree of awe.

CHAPTER 20

Lunar Nodes through the Houses

What follows are brief descriptions of how the Lunar Nodes function in the astrological houses. As was explained in chapter 16, the house containing the South Node represents talents and habits carried over from a past life. These attributes may come easily to you, but they will not advance your spiritual development. The North Node, on the other hand, represents the new territory that you need to explore in this life. These issues may challenge you, but learning to deal with them effectively will help you advance on a spiritual level.

Keep in mind that we are talking about movement and change in your spiritual life. The issues described here may not have anything to do with your career, love life, or other outwardly directed activities. Those are more likely to be described by the rest of the horoscope. On a purely technical level, also keep in mind that house placements of the Nodes can change depending on which house system you use.

The South Node in the First House
with the North Node in the Seventh

You might be quite comfortable on your own, thinking that it's all about you, but you are never going to feel spiritually whole until you find the joy and take on the burden of having another person in your life. This does not mean that the process of finding that special relationship will be natural or easy for you. That will depend on the rest of your horoscope. Nor does it mean that, once you find that relationship, it will be all you dreamed it would be. The physical, earthly properties of the relationship are not what this placement describes. What is important with this arrangement of the Lunar Nodes is how that relationship and the process of finding it fulfill the spiritual mission you have been given.

The South Node in the Second House
with the North Node in the Eighth

You know you have a lot to give in both the physical realm and the spiritual realm. And yet, there's a part of you that wants to keep it all to yourself—all your love, all your money, all your attention, and all your time. Of course, there's another part of you that knows that, no matter how determined you are to hold on to these things, at some point your grip on them is going to be broken, if by nothing else, then by death. Your spiritual health depends on you facing the inevitability of those changes. Once you have done that and have accepted the temporary nature of even your spiritual gifts, then giving of yourself will cease to be a burden. Instead, you will see it as an investment in the future of your everlasting soul.

The South Node in the Third House
with the North Node in the Ninth

At a spiritual level, at least, you are probably most at ease when you are dealing with the immediate and the routine. You see your spiritual health as being interwoven with these everyday affairs, and therefore you value the time you spend attending to them. In some cases, depending on the rest of your horoscope, you might become quite skilled in dealing with these matters and earn praise for your expertise. However, your future lies in accepting the challenge of a broader perspective on an intellectual, social, and spiritual level. There's no guarantee that you will excel in this new territory. You may stumble and feel out of place. Your ego might be bruised, but your spirit will eventually learn to soar.

The South Node in the Fourth House with the North Node in the Tenth

The past has a hold on you. It may hold you to its warm bosom like a loving mother, or it might be attached to your ankle like a ball and chain. Either way, it can interfere with your spiritual growth. You could waste your life dealing with these issues from your childhood, but you know that's not what it's all about. You know that at some point you will have to put aside the fetters of your family story and join the hurly-burly of the world. How easy or hard this journey out your front door might be will depend on the rest of your horoscope, as does the level of success and recognition you attain. What's important with this placement is what these worldly struggles teach you on a spiritual level.

The South Node in the Fifth House with the North Node in the Eleventh

You find spiritual satisfaction in the amazing things you can do. Maybe you make art. Maybe you make babies. Maybe you just make other people happy. This should be enough for anyone's spiritual well-being. Right? Then why do you sometimes get this claustrophobic feeling that you are running out of options? Maybe you do need more than your creativity. Maybe you need to surrender a bit of your precious autonomy to the will of a group or cause. Those interactions might, at times, cramp your creative instincts, and you may not appreciate the political games that come with being part of something larger than yourself, but the payback in terms of your spiritual health will be worth it.

The South Node in the Sixth House with the North Node in the Twelfth

Your spiritual comfort zone is within the world of practical matters, the art of getting things done, making arrangements, and negotiating the twists and turns of everyday life. But there's another side of life that is calling your spiritual self. It lies beyond the safety of your skills and abilities in a mysterious place that frightens you. You're not sure why this other side frightens you so. Maybe it's because it seems dark and unknowable. Maybe it's because it seems to promise you the kind of hardship and confinement you've always sought to avoid. However, surprisingly enough, it could well be within that hardship, that confinement, that dark and dreadful place, where you will find the spiritual fulfillment that has been calling your name for so long.

The South Node in the Seventh House with the North Node in the First

You get love, affection, and validation from a significant other who helps you sustain your spiritual life. Maybe the presence of this person in your life gives you a reason to feel proud or happy. Maybe they have an emotional hold on you that you think is unbreakable. However, as much as it might seem otherwise, that relationship is not your spiritual resting place. It's not necessarily that the relationship is bad for you, it's that your dependence on it has distracted you from the self-awareness and self-sufficiency you need to discover your own spiritual destiny. You don't have to jettison the relationship. You just have to change your dependence on it.

The South Node in the Eighth House with the North Node in the Second

There are things you need to let go of. These might be feelings of anger and outrage. They might be grudges or jealousies. They might also be a sense of obligation and real or imagined debts. Letting go of these feelings won't be easy because they seem to be enmeshed in your spiritual life, but you can do it if you change your attitude toward these dark emotions. You have to look at them in a simpler, more transactional way. Ask, "Does this feeling have value to me?" If the answer is no, you have to put it aside. Your well-being depends on your ability to separate what profits you on a spiritual level from that which can only create a spiritual deficit.

The South Node in the Ninth House with the North Node in the Third

As much as possible, you like to keep the spiritual side of your nature away from mundane reality. You seek purity, a spirituality that is free of all the nasty contaminants of real life in the real world. The problem is that, as a human being, it is impossible for you to live anywhere except in a real body in a real place in the real world. There are no other options. Your spiritual development will be greatly accelerated when you realize that all the silly, tedious, and annoying issues you now see as distracting you from your spiritual journey are, in fact, showing you the way.

The South Node in the Tenth House with the North Node in the Fourth

You dropped something on your way to nirvana. It might not seem all that important to you right now. After all, you're busy. You have a life and a future. But you're never going to get too far along on your journey until you pick that something up and deal with its contents. Those contents might be memories from your childhood. They might be insights and advice from your parents or other people from your past. You might have never seen that advice or those experiences as having value. It's only when you look at them a second time that the wisdom that was hidden there shines through, and you realize that the spiritual advancement you seek is not running ahead of you into the future—it's been patiently waiting for your attention somewhere deep in your past.

The South Node in the Eleventh House with the North Node in the Fifth

You always thought that your spiritual health depended on someone else, that finding your spiritual fulfillment was contingent on being a constructive member of your community and being useful to the cause. You felt you needed to wait for someone's permission, or perhaps wait your turn before that sense of fulfillment could come your way. Now you know better. Now you know that true spirituality cannot be the product of groupthink. It is an individual process. Now you know that it's up to you to create a path to spiritual advancement, and the only path that will work for you is one based on your inspiration, your desire, and your passion.

The South Node in the Twelfth House with the North Node in the Sixth

You see sacrifice as the key to advancing on a spiritual level, and you stand ready to give of yourself in whatever way is required. You accept confinement, you accept struggle, you accept being seen as less than you really are as part of your spiritual education. And yet, all your struggle and sacrifice seem to get you nowhere. Maybe the real key is to pay less attention to your own spiritual advancement and more to the well-being of others. These others might seem lost to you. They might seem completely involved by the trifling problems of everyday life. But they still need your attention, your help, your skill, and your wisdom. You might just find that giving of yourself in mundane acts of service is the only sacrifice that really counts.

CHAPTER 21

Lunar Nodes through the Signs

The way the Nodes of the Moon function in the signs is similar to the way they function in the houses. The South Node represents baggage carried over from a past life that can hold you back in terms of your spiritual development, while the North Node represents the challenges that you need to meet in this life.

The South Node in Aries with the North Node in Libra

You are moving from "me" to "we." You were born with a sense that you had to work out your spiritual destiny on your own, that there was no one around who would be able to help you. Look again, however, and you just might find that the world is full of people waiting to come to your aid. You just have to have the courage to politely ask them.

The South Node in Taurus with the North Node in Scorpio

You feel you can relax and that you have all the spiritual resources you need stored away in your religion, philosophy, or spiritual practice. Yet, deep within your psyche, doubts are percolating. You've put off addressing these doubts because you see no definite way to answer them, but the answers aren't important. What's important is putting aside your complacency and asking the questions.

The South Node in Gemini
with the North Node in Sagittarius

You keep moving. You have a snappy answer for any question that arises with regard to your spiritual needs, and you don't stick around to talk about the details. Then you get to a place where your snappy answers don't seem to apply, and you find yourself staring with awe at a broad, distant horizon and wondering why you never stopped to savor this wondrous feeling before.

The South Node in Cancer
with the North Node in Capricorn

You find peace in the spiritual connections you enjoy with your family and in the memories from your upbringing. As long as these bonds are strong, you feel secure. However, the practical demands of living in the real world often strain those relationships and test those bonds. You need to base your security on something more structured and oriented toward the future than your emotional connections with the past.

The South Node in Leo
with the North Node in Aquarius

The spiritual practices that work for other people just won't work for you. Your needs and your spirituality are special. However, waiting for a message from beyond meant just for you might not be the best approach. You are special, but not that special. Listen to the advice of your friends and find your spiritual happy place in their company.

The South Node in Virgo
with the North Node in Pisces

You weave your spirituality into the fabric of your everyday life—what you eat, how you dress, where you go, and how you get there. It becomes part of your routine. However, your real spiritual breakthroughs will not come out of the humdrum. They will come to you in dreams and visions. Make sure you're ready for them.

The South Node in Libra
with the North Node in Aries

You tend to be agreeable when it comes to spiritual matters. What everyone else is doing is fine. You don't want to be the negative one. However, you also feel that what everyone else is doing is never quite enough. You long for more intensity, more impact. At some point, you will have to stop thinking about what everyone else wants and follow your own instincts.

The South Node in Scorpio
with the North Node in Taurus

You know that there is a deep and powerful spirituality hiding somewhere within the folds and crevices of your complex psychological makeup and you've spent a lot of time looking for it. But what if that spiritual epiphany is not hiding? What if it's been standing right there in front of you this whole time—solid, simple, and just waiting for you to reach out and touch it?

The South Node in Sagittarius
with the North Node in Gemini

You are on a spiritual quest. You want to go everywhere and try all the options. There's nothing wrong with learning all you can, but getting a little out of a lot is never going to satisfy you. You need to apply your curiosity to the one thing that works best for you and get from that spiritual practice or system all it has to give.

The South Node in Capricorn
with the North Node in Cancer

You've got a system when it comes to your spiritual health. You've built it by putting together the methods recommended to you by your peers, and it seems quite efficient. However, instead of boosting your spirituality, that system might actually be the place you go to hide from it. Instead of listening to the voice of authority, maybe you should follow your feelings. They will take you where you need to go.

The South Node in Aquarius with the North Node in Leo

You're not so sure about this spirituality business. It seems so selfish and anti-social. Instead of something that lifts you up, you seek truths that will uplift your community, your people, and your world. Unfortunately, those great truths are eventually going to leave you feeling cheated. You need a truth that is totally your own, that is specific to your needs and your intellect.

The South Node in Pisces with the North Node in Virgo

You know that you are close. You feel the presence of the gods, the universe, and the all-powerful, and yet your awareness of them is indefinite and without recognizable features. What you may need to do is stop thinking about the powers that are beyond your knowledge and start paying attention to where you are right now. The shape of the divine might actually be found in the simple operations of your everyday life.

★ ★ ★

These descriptions of the Nodes of the Moon in the signs have been written in a way that complements rather than conflicts with the descriptions of the Nodes in the houses. However, if you were born with a horoscope in which the signs and houses are reversed so that the South Node is in Libra in the First House and so on, there still might be some confusion. Remember that the house positions of the two Nodes describe the functions or areas of life in which your personal spiritual journey is most likely to be focused, while the signs reveal the attributes of your personality or character that will be highlighted.

CHAPTER 22

The Transiting Aspects

I n chapter 17, we saw that transiting aspects involving the Nodes of the Moon seem to bring us messages from a place beyond our day-to-day reality. What follows is a summary of the kind of messages you might expect to come to you when the transiting Nodes of the Moon aspect planets or placements in your natal horoscope or when transiting planets aspect your natal Lunar Nodes. Keep in mind that the impact these messages have and your response to them will depend on many factors. One of these is how aware and attentive you are of your spiritual life. Another is how ready you are for that message. Often the messages that come to us through the portals represented by the Nodes of the Moon get lost in the immediacies of living. We are not faulted for missing these messages. Aspects involving the Lunar Nodes are happening all the time. The message you miss today could be repeated at a later date, perhaps when you are in a better frame of mind or spirit to receive it.

Aspects Involving the Sun and the Lunar Nodes

The Nodes of the Moon are calling to the Hero within you. For some of you, this will mean standing up for your principles. For others, it will mean showing courage and fortitude in fraught situations or putting your well-being on the line for the sake of someone else. The issue might be big, or it might be small, depending on what is going on in your life at the time this transit occurs. The call will always be for the best and strongest elements of your character to come forward.

In most cases, this is a positive transit. However, if the message comes at a time when you are feeling less than heroic, when your self-image is at a low point and you lack confidence in your ability to meet the challenges set before you, this call can be painful to hear, and you may want to run away from it. Also, there are times when it is just not practical to answer this call, when you lack the resources or abilities necessary to play the role of Hero. Failing to answer this call may leave you feeling guilty and regretful, but sometimes the purpose of this call is to make you aware there are limitations to what any Hero can do.

Aspects Involving the Moon and the Lunar Nodes

These transits often coincide with periods when you are made to feel vulnerable and/or dependent on the judgments and actions of other people. It is as if you are being called to surrender yourself to fate or to powers beyond your control. Depending on other factors, both in your natal horoscope and in your life, this might seem like a long-awaited release. On the other hand, it might also seem as if your life is being hijacked and your will trampled.

Aspects by the transiting Moon to your natal Nodes of the Moon (squares and conjunctions) are more or less a weekly event. Their importance to your spiritual life would seem to be minimal. Aspects by the transiting Nodes to your natal Moon, however, occur every two or three years. Because they are so intertwined with your emotions and the irrational, the messages these transits carry can at times be especially poignant, but that emotional impact will likely be apparent to you alone.

Aspects Involving Mercury and the Lunar Nodes

Speak! You know you have something to say. The message with this transit is that it's time to say it. Keep your eyes open and your mind alert. What needs to be said will probably come out of things in your immediate environment. You just have to winnow through all the distractions and irrelevant details. You may also have prejudices, attitudes, and assumptions that can further separate you from the information you need and muddle what you have to say. These transits can become periods of intellectual struggle in which you are forced to put aside cherished preconceptions and see the world as it really is.

There are times with these transits when what you have to say has great power. It can change your life. There are other times when it will be more personal, something you have to say that only has relevance to your spiritual awareness. And sometimes what you have to say could get lost in the detritus of information that is constantly coming at us through social media and the twenty-four-hour news cycle. You want to speak, but your voice is drowned out. That's okay. Mercury and the Nodes keep on moving. They will meet again, and this time, you'll be ready.

Aspects Involving Venus and the Lunar Nodes

With these aspects, the message often has to do with your connections to other people. You are called upon to recognize the importance of those relationships to your spiritual well-being. These aspects can signal a period in which you celebrate relationships and the people dear to you. However, they can also bring us periods of mourning in which your link to another person is severed. This could be because of a separation, a divorce, or even a death. The absence of the relationship and the gap that is left behind reveal their importance.

On the other hand, there are some relationships that need to be ended, relationships that may be holding back your spiritual development. In these instances, the message brought to you by this aspect is that it is time to say goodbye. The process of doing this might be difficult and heartrending. It may reveal things about the relationship that you would rather not acknowledge, but, in the end, answering this call will make you more, not less, complete.

Aspects Involving Mars and the Lunar Nodes

These aspects might seem a little scary, particularly considering the kinds of mundane events (as noted in chapter 17) that often accompany them. However, the influence of aspects between Mars and the Nodes of the Moon in natal charts seems to be more benign. Often it is just a matter of sharpening our competitive edge and reminding us that winning isn't just about physical and intellectual attributes. Winning is also about being spiritually aligned with the moment in which you are living. While on a physical level, winning might be a struggle, on a spiritual level, you are simply unpacking a potential that was already there.

At the same time, you shouldn't sleep on these transits. In certain instances, particularly when you are undergoing another stressful transit, these aspects can act as triggers that release pent-up angst and anger, feelings that can both disrupt your physical existence and sour your spiritual life. Once again, it is a matter of unpacking a potential that has already been established, but now it is the potential for confrontation and conflict.

Aspects Involving Jupiter and the Lunar Nodes

With these transits, you are given the opportunity to display or act on your faith. This might be your faith in a deity or in a philosophical principle or in a political theory or simply in your own inner strength or good fortune. Hearing this message and answering it can, in some cases, have extremely positive results. Two people among my celebrity examples were able to kick a long-standing drug addiction during a transit of Jupiter by the Nodes of the Moon. Faith can be a powerful force, and sometimes it can lead us to the promised land.

But there are also instances in which our faith is misplaced, and the promised land is an illusion. There is no guarantee that the call to display your faith will present you with a clear, black-and-white choice. The circumstances surrounding your act of faith might be complex and not at all pleasant. It might seem less like a call than a challenge. That challenge can have special relevance to your spiritual life and the belief systems that supports it. Real faith is not blind. It is the product of wisdom and learning. Along with bringing your faith into the foreground, these transits can also expose the weaknesses and fallacies of that faith.

Aspects Involving Saturn and the Lunar Nodes

Where Jupiter aspecting the Nodes of the Moon brings us faith, Saturn brings us doubt. This could be doubt in yourself—your talents, your abilities, your appearance, or your intelligence. It could also be doubt in the way you are living and in the choices you have made. The events that bring you the message of doubt can be traumatic, but they can also be subtle and seemingly innocuous. In either case, the true significance of this will be felt on a personal and spiritual level.

These transits are not always bleak occasions. Doubt serves a purpose. It keeps us asking questions about the beliefs and presumptions on which our spiritual life is based. This is the Teacher at work, pushing us to find answers to these questions. Those answers allow us to grow both on a spiritual and an intellectual level. During these transits, you might feel called to take a critical look at your life and remove from it those things that are impeding your spiritual and personal development. These transits don't have to only be about saying no to yourself or to life in general. They can also be a means of liberating yourself from ideas, habits, and relationships in which your doubt has crept ahead of your faith.

Aspects Involving Uranus and the Lunar Nodes

You expect these transits to bring drastic changes into your life, and they sometimes do, but more often the message we get with these aspects has more to do with a complete rearrangement of your expectations. Sometimes you get what you want with these aspects and then realize that it wasn't what you wanted at all. Other times you are denied the thing you wanted only to find that not having it has set you free.

Uranus transits of any sort are like earthquakes. Anything in your life that has not been properly secured is apt to be shaken loose and hit you on the head. With Uranus's transits involving the Nodes, what gets shaken loose often has to do with your spiritual life. Even when these aspects don't coincide with dramatic events, some rearranging of your approach to religion or spirituality is likely. This doesn't have to be a complete overhaul of your belief system (though it can be). It can be a sudden awareness of a weakness or contradiction in that system that gives you pause. A Uranus transit is the time to batten down those insecure notions before they come crashing down on you.

Aspects Involving Neptune and the Lunar Nodes

The message that comes to us with this transit to the Nodes of the Moon often has the mystical, irrational quality of a Vision. These messages can be glorious (think of Bernadette and her vision of Mary), but they're not always true. This is particularly the case when the message tells you something you badly want to hear. A transcendent vision that is tainted by subjective need will almost always deceive you and leave promises unfulfilled.

We think of visions as showing us positive things, but that is not always the case. Sometimes the visions you have under these transits are of yourself as a failure. Such a Vision has typically been tainted by your own insecurities and fear and is therefore utterly false, but if you choose to believe this vison and act on it, the results are likely to fulfill just what this bleak vision promises. Approach these transits with care, and be mindful that they can bring out both the strongest and the weakest elements of your character.

Aspects Involving Pluto and the Lunar Nodes

With these transits, we are often faced with the inevitable. The doors that you knew—or at least strongly suspected—were going to be closed to you slam shut, and you have to deal with the consequences. In many cases, the finality that comes with these transits is a relief. Now you know exactly where we stand, and you are no longer distracted by false hopes. Still, these messages are rarely received with joy.

Pluto transits involving the Nodes of the Moon have a way of showing us where our egos and our desire for control and power are interfering with our spiritual health and development. Dealing with such issues typically demands a lot of self-examination and internal work. It can be a complex and painful process, one that leaves us feeling demeaned and psychologically exposed.

But, as always with Pluto, what it takes away in terms of pride and ego makes room for new growth and deeper understanding.

Aspects Involving the Natal Lunar Nodes with the Transiting Lunar Nodes

Here we have the alignment of two gateways. Without an archetype to define it, what passes through them is difficult to discern. Still, we need to pay close attention to what happens to us during these transits. The events or, sometimes, lack of events that coincide with these transits can often tell us much about the intricate interplay of choice and fate in our lives.

It might be helpful to think of these nodal returns and nodal squares in the same way you think of taking your car into the shop for regular maintenance. Just as these maintenance checks usually include a wheel alignment, these aspects between the Nodes represent a regular check of the alignment of your spiritual life. Most of the time after the work is done on your car, you drive away without noticing a difference. But sometimes the mechanic finds problems with your vehicle that require your immediate attention. Likewise, there are times in which these transits necessitate a major realignment of your spiritual existence with the larger spiritual world. This realignment might be accompanied by serious disruptions in your life, but they are necessary.

Aspects Involving the Ascendant/Descendant Axis and the Transiting Lunar Nodes

With these transits, issues involving your relationships often crop up. It isn't just about other people. It's also about how changes in those relationships change your identity and self-image. Again, the Nodes of the Moon act as a gateway, bringing issues of fate and possibly past life connections into play. This doesn't necessarily mean that the relationship in question is related to past life experiences, but it does indicate that whatever is happening has a deeper spiritual meaning to you.

Aspects Involving the Midheaven/IC Axis and the Transiting Lunar Nodes

Here, the message that comes to us through the Nodes is likely to relate to your career. It might be a whisper from out of the blue that shows you a new opportunity, or it might be a failure that reveals a lack of preparation. It could also be the realization that what you're doing brings you no joy. These transits are neither good nor bad, but they are valuable for the information they give us about how our career aspirations align with our spiritual well-being.

Sources

Aaron, Henry, and Lonnie Wheeler. *I Had a Hammer: The Hank Aaron Story*. New York: Harper Collins, 1991.

Abraham, Yvonne. "At 80, Schlafly Is Still a Conservative Force." *Boston Globe*, September 2, 2004. www.boston.com/news/nation /articles/2004/09/02/at_80_schlafly_is_still_a_conservative_force/.

Ackroyd, Thomas. *The Life of Thomas More*. New York: Anchor Books, 1998.

Adams, Rebecca. "Sarah Ferguson Goes from Princess Diana's Sidekick to Single Woman." *Huffington Post*, October 15, 2012. https://www.huffpost .com/entry/sarah-ferguson-style-photos-pictures-birthday_n_1955776.

"Al Gore Biography." Biography. Last modified May 12, 2020. https://www.biography.com/political-figure/al-gore.

Amburn, Ellis. *Pearl: The Obsessions and Passions of Janis Joplin: A Biography*. New York: Warner Books, 1992.

"Angela Davis." History. Last modified January 16, 2020. https://www .history.com/topics/black-history/angela-davis.

Baatz, Simon. *For the Thrill of It: Leopold, Loeb, and the Murder That Shocked Chicago*. New York: Harper Collins Publishers, 2008.

Baldwin, Lewis V. *Behind the Public Veil: The Humanness of Martin Luther King, Jr.* Minneapolis: Fortress Press, 2016.

Baxter, John. *Steven Spielberg: The Unauthorized Biography*. New York: Harper Collins, 1996.

Bego, Mark. *Tina Turner: Break Every Rule*. Lanham, MD: Taylor Trade Publishing, 2003.

Berle, Milton, and Haskel Frankel. *Milton Berle: An Autobiography*. New York: Applause Theater and Cinema Books, 1974.

Berman, Larry. *Lyndon Johnson's War: The Road to Stalemate in Vietnam*. New York: W. W. Norton, 1989.

"Bernadette Soubirous." Wikipedia. Last modified August 8, 2021. https://en.wikipedia.org/wiki/Bernadette_Soubirous.

Blue, Adrianne. *Martina: The Lives and Times of Martina Navratilova*. New York: Carol Publishing Company, 1995.

"Bob Geldof." Wikipedia. Last modified August 7, 2021. https://en.wikipedia.org/wiki/Bob_Geldof.

Bono, Chaz, and Billie Firzpatrick. *Transition: The Story of How I Became a Man*. New York: Dutton, 2011.

Brady, Frank. *Endgame: Bobby Fischer's Remarkable Rise and Fall—From America's Brightest Prodigy to the Edge of Madness*. New York: Crown Publishers, 2011.

Brands, H. W. *Traitor to His Class: The Privileged Life and Radical Presidency of Franklin Delano Roosevelt*. New York: Doubleday, 2008.

Brevin, Jess. *Squeaky: The Life and Times of Lynette Alice Fromme*. New York: Buzz Books, 1997.

Brodie, Fawn M. *The Devil Drives: A Life of Sir Richard Burton*. New York: W. W. Norton and Company, 1967.

Brown, Julie K. "How a Future Trump Cabinet Member Gave a Serial Sex Abuser the Deal of a Lifetime." *Miami Herald*, November 28, 2018. https://www.miamiherald.com/news/local/article220097825.html.

Bryan, John. *This Soldier Still at War.* New York: Harcourt Brace Jovanovich, 1975.

Bueno, Antoinette. "Whoopi Goldberg Talks About Her Future on the View." *ET*, May 8, 2020. https://www.etonline.com/whoopi-goldberg -talks-about-her-future-on-the-view-146234.

Bugliosi, Vincent, and Curt Gentry. *Helter Skelter: The Story of the Manson Murders.* New York: W. W. Norton & Company, 1974.

"A Byte Out of History: The Patty Hearst Kidnapping." *The FBI.* Last modified February 2009. https://archives.fbi.gov/archives/news/stories/2009 /february/hearst_020409.

Bytwerk, Randall. *Julius Streicher.* New York: Stein and Day, 1983.

"Caitlyn Jenner." *Wikipedia.* Last modified August 10, 2021. https://en .wikipedia.org/wiki/Caitlyn_Jenner.

Carlin, Peter Ames. *Bruce.* New York: Simon and Schuster, 2012.

Carlisle, Belinda. *Lips Unsealed: A Memoir.* New York: Crown Publishers, 2010.

Chafe, William H. *Bill and Hillary: The Politics of the Personal.* New York: Farrar, Straus, and Giroux, 2012.

"Charles Atlas." *Wikipedia.* Last modified July 12, 2021. https://en.wikipedia .org/wiki/Charles_Atlas.

Charters, Ann. *Kerouac.* New York: St. Martin's Press, 1994.

Chipp, Isaac. "Jack Nicklaus, 'I Underachieved All My Life.'" *USA Today*, June 4, 2015. ffw.usatodya.com/2015/06/jack-nicklaus-i-underachived-all-my-life.

Clarke, Gerald. *Capote: A Biography.* New York: Simon and Schuster, 1988.

Cleugh, James. *The First Masochist: A Biography of Leopold von Sacher-Masoch.* New York: Stein and Day, 1967.

Cohen, Morton N. *Lewis Carroll: A Biography.* New York: Alfred A. Knopf, 1995.

Cohodas, Nadine. *Princess Noire: The Tumultuous Reign of Nina Simone.* New York: Pantheon Books, 2010.

Comella, Lynn. "Nina Hartley's Adult Film Career Has Been Long, Distinguished, and Trailblazing—and It's Far from Over." *Las Vegas*

Weekly, October 6, 2010. https://lasvegasweekly.com/as-we-see-it/2010 /oct/06/nina-hartleys-adult-film-career-has-been-long-dist/.

Crosby, David, and Carl Gottlieb. *Long Time Gone: The Autobiography of David Crosby*. New York: Doubleday, 1988.

Cryer, Jon. "Jon Cryer Reveals the Inside Account of Charlie Sheen's Infamous Meltdown." *Hollywood Reporter*, March 18, 2015. www.hollywood reporter.com/news/jon-cryer-reveals-inside-insane-782410.

Davis, J. D. *Unconquered: The Saga of Cousins, Jerry Lee Lewis, Jimmy Swaggart, and Mickey Gilley*. Dallas, TX: Brown Books, 2012.

Deezen, Eddie. "Did Wilt Chamberlain Really Sleep With 20,000 Women?" *Mental Floss*. Last modified February 6, 2018. https://www.mentalfloss .com/article/12310/did-wilt-chamberlain-really-sleep-20000-women.

de Jorge, Alex. *Baudelaire: Prince of Clouds*. New York: Paddington Press, 1976.

"Divine (Performer)." *Wikipedia*. Last modified August 8, 2021. https://en.wikipedia.org/wiki/Divine_(performer).

Docter, Richard. *Becoming a Woman: A Biography of Christine Jorgensen*. New York: The Harworth Press, 2008.

Donohoe, Ellie May. "Susan Boyle, 58, Wears Her Iconic Britain's Got Talent Gold Audition Dress ELEVEN Years after Rising to Fame on the ITV Show." *Daily Mail*, March 6, 2020. https://www.dailymail.co.uk/tvshow biz/article-8085089/Susan-Boyle-dons-iconic-Britains-Got-Talent -audition-dress-11-years-later.html.

Dugard, Jaycee. *A Stolen Life: Memoirs*. New York: Simon Schuster, 2011.

"Eric Harris and Dylan Klebold." *Wikipedia*. Last modified July 21, 2021. https://en.wikipedia.org/wiki/Eric_Harris_and_Dylan_Klebold.

Fahs, Breanne. *Valerie Solanas: The Defiant Life of the Woman Who Wrote* Scum *(and Shot Andy Warhol)*. New York: The Feminist Press at the City of New York University, 2014.

Filkins, Dexter. "Shot in the Heart." *New Yorker*, October 26, 2015. https:// www.newyorker.com/magazine/2015/10/26/shot-in-the-heart.

Finn, Natalie. "The Weird, Wild and Tragically Short Life of Anna Nicole Smith." *ENews*, November 28, 2019. https://www.eonline.com/news /896532/the-weird-wild-and-tragically-short-life-of-anna-nicole-smith.

Fisher, Carrie. *Wishful Drinking*. New York: Simon and Schuster, 2008.

Fletcher, Alex. "Brigitte Nielsen Signs for 'I'm a Celebrity'?" *Digital Spy*. Last modified February 27, 2012. www.digitalspy.com/british-tv/s100 /im-a-celebrity-uk/news/a368101/brigitte-nielsen-sings-for-im-a-celebrity .tml.

"Former Master Champion George Archer Battled Secret Lifelong Illiteracy, Moving First Person Account Written by Archer's Wife Appears in the March/April Issue of Golf for Women." *Business Wire*, February 14, 2006. https://www.businesswire.com/news/home/20060214005850/en /Masters-Champion-George-Archer-Battled-Secret-Life-long.

Foster, Richard. *The Real Bettie Page: The Truth About the Queen of Pinups*. New York: Citadel Press, 1997.

Fox, Michael J. *Always Looking Up: The Adventures of an Incurable Optimist*. New York: Hyperion, 2008.

Fraser, Antonia. *Marie Antoinette: The Journey*. New York: Doubleday, 2001.

Fraser, David. *Knight's Cross: A Life of Field Marshal Erwin Rommel*. New York: Harper Collins, 1993.

Friedman, Lawrence. *The Lives of Erich Fromm: Love's Prophet*. New York: Columbia University Press, 2013.

Gabler, Neal. *Walt Disney: The Triumph of the American Imagination*. New York: Vintage Books, 2006.

"George Michael 1963–2016." *Biography*. Last modified October 22, 2019. https://www.biography.com/musician/george-michael.

Goldsmith, Barbara. *Obsessive Genius: The Inner World of Marie Curie*. New York: W. W. Norton & Company, 2005.

Goodstein, Laurie. "Billy Graham, 99, Dies; Pastor Filled Stadiums and Counseled Presidents." *New York Times*, February 21, 2018. https://www .nytimes.com/2018/02/21/obituaries/billy-graham-dead.html.

Goodwin, Doris Kearns. *Team of Rivals: The Political Genius of Abraham Lincoln*. New York: Simon and Schuster, 2005.

Görtemaker, Heike B. *Eva Braun: Life with Hitler*. Translated by Damion Searls. New York: Alfred A. Knopf, 2011.

Green, Douglas B. *Singing in the Saddle: The History of the Singing Cowboy*. Nashville: The Country Music Foundation Press, 2002.

Greenberg, Andy. *This Machine Kills Secrets: How WikiLeakers, Cypherpunks, and Hacktivists Aim to Free the World's Information*. New York: Dutton, 2012.

Grey, Rudolph. *Nightmare of Ecstasy: The Life and Art of Edward D. Wood Jr.* Port Townsend, WA: Feral House, 1992.

Grohmann, Will. *E. L. Kirchner*. New York: Arts, 1961.

Grosskurth, Phyllis. *Havelock Ellis: A Biography*. New York: New York University Press, 1985.

Guy, John. *The True Life of Mary Stuart, Queen of Scots*. New York: Houghton Mifflin Company, 2004.

Halperin, Ian. *Whitney and Bobbi Kristina: The Deadly Price of Fame*. New York: Gallery Books, 2015.

Harrington, Walt. "George Bush: World War II Navy Pilot." *Hstorynet*. Last modified June 26, 2007. https://www.historynet.com/george-hw-bush.

Hatfield, Larry D. "Anton LaVey, Church of Satan Founder (Obituaries)." *San Francisco Chronicle*, November 7, 1997. https://www.sfchronicle.com/.

"Heather Locklear." *Wikipedia*. Last modified July 20, 2021. https://en.wikipedia.org/wiki/Heather_Locklear.

Heilbrun, Carolyn G. *The Education of a Woman: The Life of Gloria Steinem*. New York: Dial Press, 1995.

"Henry Ford." *History*. March 26, 2020. https://www.history.com/topics/inventions/henry-ford.

Herman, Eleanor. *Sex with Kings: 500 Years of Adultery, Power, Rivalry, and Revenge*. New York: Harper Collins, 2004.

Herrera, Hayden. *Frida: A Biography of Frida Kahlo.* New York: Harper Perennial, 2002.

Higgins, Michael W. *Heretic Blood: The Spiritual Geography of Thomas Merton.* New York: Stoddart Publishing Company, 1998.

History.com Editors. "This Day in History: September 10, 1977: Serial Killers Charlene Williams and Gerald Galego Meet." *History.* Last modified November 13, 2009. https://www.history.com/this-day-in-history/serial-killing-couple-meets.

Hodges, Andrew. *Alan Turing: The Enigma.* New York: Simon and Schuster, 1983.

Hoffman, Robert L. *More Than a Trial: The Struggle over Captain Dreyfus.* New York: Free Press, 1980.

Howe, Ellic. *Astrology: A Recent History Including the Untold Story of Its Role in World War II.* New York: Walker and Company, 1967.

Howe, Russell Warren. *Mata Hari: The True Story.* New York: Dodd, Mead, and Company, 1986.

Hubner, John. *Bottom Feeders: From Free Love to Hard Core, the Rise and Fall of Counterculture Gurus Jim and Artie Mitchell.* New York: Doubleday, 1992.

Hunt, Tristram. *Marx's General: The Revolutionary Life of Friedrich Engels.* New York: Metropolitan Books, 2009.

Hyman, Timothy. *Bonnard.* London: Thames and Hudson, 1998.

"John Derek, 71, Actor Known as Wife's Svengali, Is Dead." *New York Times,* May 24, 1998. www.nytimes.com/1998/05/24/nyregion/john-derek-71-actor-known-as-wife-s-svengali-is-dead.html.

Jones, Lesley-Ann. *Hero: David Bowie.* London: Hodder and Stoughton, 2016.

Jordan, David. *The Revolutionary Career of Maximilien Robespierre.* New York: The Free Press, 1985.

Kaplan, James. *Frank: The Voice.* New York: Doubleday, 2010.

Kaufman, Michael T. "Stokely Carmichael, Rights Leader Who Coined 'Black Power,' Dies at 57." *New York Times,* November 16, 1998.

https://www.nytimes.com/1998/11/16/us/stokely-carmichael-rights
-leader-who-coined-black-power-dies-at-57.html.

Keogh, Pamela Clarke. *Elvis Presley: The Man, the Life, the Legend.* New York: Atria Books, 2004.

Kershaw, Ian. *Hitler: A Biography.* New York: W. W. Norton, 2010.

Ketchum, Richard M. *Will Rogers: His Life and Times.* New York: American Heritage Publishing, 1973.

Kilduff, Peter. *Richthofen: Beyond the Legend of the Red Baron.* New York: John Wiley & Sons, 1993.

King, Stephen. *On Writing: A Memoir of the Craft.* New York: Scribners, 2000.

Klein, Edward. *All Too Human: The Love Story of Jack and Jackie Kennedy.* New York: Pocket Books, 1996.

Klein, Edward. *Katie: The Real Story.* New York: Crown Publishers, 2007.

Klein, Edward. *Ted Kennedy: The Dream that Never Died.* New York: Crown Publishers, 2009.

Kluger, Jeffrey. *Splendid Solution: Jonas Salk and the Conquest of Polio.* New York: G. P. Putnam's Sons, 2004.

Knopp, Guido. *Hitler's Henchmen.* Translated by Angus McGeoch. Phoenix Mill, UK: Sutton, 1996.

Kramer, Peter D. *Freud: Inventor of the Modern Mind.* New York: Harper Collins, 2006.

Krohn, Katherine. *Oprah Winfrey.* Minneapolis: Lerner Publications, 2005.

"Kurt Weill." *Music and the Holocaust.* Accessed July 19, 2021. http://holocaustmusic.ort.org/politics-and-propaganda/third-reich/weill-kurt/.

Lardner, Ring Jr. *I'd Hate Myself in the Morning: A Memoir.* New York: Thunder's Mouth Press, 2000.

"Lena Horne Obituary." *Guardian,* May 10, 2010. https://www.theguardian.com/music/2010/may/10/lena-horne-obituary.

Lever, Maurice. *Sade: A Biography.* Translated by Arthur Goldhammer. New York: Farrar, 1993.

Levitt, Shelley. "River's End." *People Magazine,* November 15, 1993.

Levron, Jacque. *Pompadour.* Translated by Claire Eliane Engel. New York: St. Martin's Press, 1961.

Liukkonen, Petri. "Simone Weil." *Internet Archive.* Last modified 2004. https://web.archive.org/web/20070424181411/http://www.kirjasto.sci.fi/weil.htm.

Longerich, Peter. *Goebbels: A Biography.* Translated by Alan Bance, Jeremy Noakes, and Lesley Sharpe. New York: Random House, 2015.

"Lucky Luciano." *The Mob Museum.* Accessed July 20, 2021. https://themobmuseum.org/notable_names/lucky-luciano/.

Magida, Arthur J. *Prophet of Rage: A Life of Louis Farrakhan and His Nation.* New York: Basic Books, 1996.

Margolick, David. *Beyond Glory: Joe Louis vs. Max Schmeling and a World on the Brink.* New York: Alfred Knopf, 2005.

Markus, Julia. *Dared and Done: The Marriage of Elizabeth Barrett and Robert Browning.* New York: Alfred A. Knopf, 1995.

Marshall, George, and David Polng. *Schweitzer: A Biography.* Garden City, NY: Doubleday and Company, 1971.

Martin, Justin. *Nader: Crusader, Spoiler, Icon.* Cambridge, MA: Perseus Publishing, 2002.

Martinez, Christina Catherine. "Jim Carrey's Cartoons Reflect the Political Circus That Inspires Them." *CNN Style.* Last modified December 4, 2018. https://www.cnn.com/style/article/jim-carrey-trump-political-cartoons/index.html.

Marwell, David G. *Mengele: Unmasking the Angel of Death.* New York: W. W. Norton and Company, 2020.

Matera, Dary. *John Dillinger: The Life and Death of America's First Celebrity Criminal.* New York: Carroll and Graf Publishers, 2004.

Maurois, Andre. *Byron.* New York: D. Appleton & Company, 1957.

McDonough, Jimmy. *Big Bosoms and Square Jaws: The Biography of Russ Meyer, King of the Sex Film.* New York: Crown Publishers, 2005.

McGilligan, Patrick. *Clint: The Life and Legend*. New York: St. Martin's Press, 1999.

McGillivary, David. "Linda Lovelace." *Guardian*, April 23, 2002. https://www.theguardian.com/news/2002/apr/24/guardianobituaries.filmnews.

Michel, Lou, and Dan Herbeck. *American Terrorist: Timothy McVeigh and the Oklahoma City Bombing*. New York: Regan Books, 2001.

Miller, Arthur I. *Deciphering the Cosmic Number: The Strange Friendship of Wolfgang Pauli and Carl Jung*. New York: W. W. Norton, 2009.

Miller, William D. *Dorothy Day: A Biography*. San Francisco: Harper and Row, 1982.

Moore, Michael. *Here Comes Trouble: Stories from My Life*. New York: Grand Central Publishing, 2011.

Morgan, Ted. *Churchill: Young Man in a Hurry, 1874–1915*. New York: Simon and Schuster, 1982.

Morris, Kenneth E. *Jimmy Carter: American Moralist*. Athens, GA: University of Georgia Press, 1996.

Munson, Richard. *Tesla: Inventor of the Modern*. New York: W. W. Norton & Company, 2018.

"Myra Hindley." *Crime Museum*. Last modified 2021. https://www.crime museum.org/crime-library/serial-killers/myra-hindley/.

Naifeh, Steven Smith, and Gregory Smith. *Van Gogh: The Life*. New York: Random House, 2011.

Naipaul, Shiva. *Journey to Nowhere: A New World Tragedy*. New York: Simon and Schuster, 1980.

Nitske, Robert. *The Life of Wilhelm Conrad Röntgen: The Discoverer of the X-Ray*. Tucson, AZ: University of Arizona Press, 1971.

Oosterhuis, Harry. *Stepchildren of Nature: Krafft-Ebing, Psychiary, and the Making of Sexual Identity*. Chicago: University of Chicago Press, 2000.

Orth, Maureen. *Vulgar Favors: Andrew Cunanan, Gianni Versace, and the Largest Failed Manhunt in US History*. New York: Delacorte Press, 1999.

Osborne, Lucy. "Prince Andrew and Jeffrey Epstein: What You Need to Know." *Guardian*, December 7, 2019. https://www.theguardian.com/uk-news/2019/dec/07/prince-andrew-jeffrey-epstein-what-you-need-to-know.

Oyler, Lauren. "The Radical Style of Andrea Dworkin." *New Yorker*, March 25, 2019. https://www.newyorker.com/magazine/2019/04/01/the-radical-style-of-andrea-dworkin.

Padovr, Sual K. *The Life and Death of Louis XVI*. New York: Tapling Publishing Company, 1963.

Pavlich, Katie. "Pavlich: Where Is the Media's Explanation for Avenatti?" *The Hill*, May 28, 2019. https://thehill.com/opinion/judiciary/445857-pavlich-where-is-the-medias-explanation-for-avenatti.

Polanski, Roman. *Roman by Polanski*. New York: William Morrow and Company, 1984.

Polizzotti, Mark. *Revolution of the Mind: The Life of Andre Breton*. New York: Farrar, Straus, and Giroux, 1995.

Pomerantz, Dorothy. "Robert Downey Jr. Tops Forbes' List of Hollywood's Highest-Paid Actors." *Forbes Magazine*, July 16, 2013. https://www.forbes.com/sites/dorothypomerantz/2013/07/16/robert-downey-jr-tops-forbes-list-of-hollywoods-highest-paid-actors/#44d51048589f.

Poole, W. Scott. *In the Mountains of Madness: The Life and Extraordinary Afterlife of H. P. Lovecraft*. Berkley, CA: Soft Skull Press, 2016.

Posner, Gerald. *Case Closed: Lee Harvey Oswald and the Assassination of JFK*. New York: Random House, 1993.

Robb, Graham. *Rimbaud*. New York: W. W. Norton and Company, 2000.

Ro, Ronin. *Prince: The Music and the Masks*. New York: St. Martin's Press, 2011.

"Rodney King." *Wikipedia*. Last modified July 21, 2021. https://en.wikipedia.org/wiki/Rodney_King.

Rosenbaun, David. "George McGovern Dies at 90: Liberal Trounced but Never Silenced." *New York Times*, October 22, 2012. https://www.nytimes.com/2012/10/22/us/politics/george-mcgovern-a-democratic-presidential-nominee-and-liberal-stalwart-dies-at-90.html.

"Sam Peckinpah: Biography." *IMDB*. Accessed July 20, 2021. https://www
.imdb.com/name/nm0001603/bio?ref_=nm_ov_bio_sm.

Sandford, Christopher. *Masters of Mystery: The Strange Friendship of Arthur
Conan Doyle and Harry Houdini*. New York: Palgrave Macmillan, 2011.

Saxton, Martha. *Jayne Mansfield and the American Fifties*. Boston: Houghton
Mifflin Company, 1975.

Schmidt, Randy L. *Little Girl Blue: The Life of Karen Carpenter*. Chicago:
Chicago Review Press, 2010.

Seay, Davin. *Mick Jagger: The Story Behind the Rolling Stones*. New York:
Birch Lane Press, 1993.

Segev, Tom. *The Life and Legends of Simon Wiesenthal*. New York: Doubleday,
2010.

Seymour, Miranda. *Robert Graves: Life on the Edge*. New York: Henry Holt &
Company, 1995.

Shannon, Elaine, and Ann Blackman. *The Spy Next Door: The Extraordinary
Secret Life of Robert Philip Hanssen, the Most Damaging FBI Agent in US History*. Boston: Little, Brown, and Company, 2002.

Shattuck, Roger. *The Banquet Years: The Arts in France, 1885–1918*. New York:
Harcourt, Brace, and Company, 1958.

Shepard, Charles. *Forgiven: The Rise and Fall of Jim Bakker and the PTL Minis-
try*. New York: Atlantic Monthly Press, 1989.

Shipman, David. *Judy Garland: The Secret Life of an American Legend*.
New York: Hyperion, 1993.

Shulman, Irving. *Valentino*. New York: Trident Press, 1967.

Sides, Hampton. *Hellhound on His Trail: The Stalking of Martin Luther King Jr.
and the International Hunt for His Assassin*. New York: Doubleday, 2010.

Sieczkowski, Cavan. "Orson Scott Card Calls Backlash to Anti-Gay Views
'Savage, Lying, Deceptive Personal Attacks.'" *Huffington Post*, October 31,
2013. https://www.huffpost.com/topic/orson-scott-card-gay-marriage.

"Sigourney Weaver Biography." *IMDB*. Accessed July 19, 2021. www.imdb
/name/nm0000244/bio.

Slater, Leonard. *Aly: A Biography*. New York: Random House, 1965.

Smith, Dinitia. "One False Note in This Musician's Life: Billy Tipton Remembered with Love Even by Those Who Were Deceived." *New York Times*, June 2, 1998. https://www.nytimes.com/1998/06/02/arts/one -false-note-musician-s-life-billy-tipton-remembered-with-love-even-those -who.html.

Smith, E. A. *George IV*. New Haven, CT: Yale University Press, 1999.

Smith, Jean Edward. *Bush*. New York: Simon and Schuster, 2016.

Smith, Peter. *Doomsday Men: The Real Dr. Strangelove and the Dream of the Super Weapon*. New York: St. Martin's Press, 2007.

Smith, Sally Bedell. *Prince Charles: The Passions and Paradoxes of an Improbable Life*. New York: Random House, 2017.

Sobel, Dava. *Galileo's Daughter: A Historical Memoir of Science, Faith, and Love*. New York: Penguin Group, 1999.

"Sophia Scholl and the White Rose." *The National WWII Museum*. Last modified February 22, 2020. https://www.nationalww2museum.org/war /articles/sophie-scholl-and-white-rose.

Spoto, Donald. *Enchantment: The Life of Audrey Hepburn*. New York: Harmony Books, 2006.

Sprinkle, Annie. *Post-Porn Modernist: My 25 Years as a Multimedia Whore*. San Francisco: Cleis Press, 1998.

Stanford, Peter. "Christine Keeler Obituary: The Woman at the Heart of the Profumo Affair." *Guardian*, December 6, 2017. https://www.theguardian .com/uk-news/2017/dec/05/christine-keeler-obituary.

Stangneth, Bettina. *Eichmann Before Jerusalem: The Unexamined Life of a Mass Murderer*. New York: Alfred A. Knopf, 2011.

Stein, David. *Running Wild: A Biography of Clara Bow*. New York: Doubleday, 1988.

Stout, David. "Doctor in a Clown Suit Battles Ills of His Profession." *New York Times*, December 15, 1998. www.nytimes.com/learning /teachers/featured_articles/19981215tuesday.html.

Strouse, Jean. *Morgan: America's Financier*. New York: Random House, 1999.

Sullivan, Caroline. "Amy Winehouse Obituary." *Guardian*, July 23, 2011. https://www.theguardian.com/music/2011/jul/23/amy-winehouse-obituary.

Swenson, Karen. *Greta Garbo: A Life Apart*. New York: Scribner, 1997.

Taraborrelli, J. Randy. *The Secret Life of Marilyn Monroe*. New York: Grand Central Publishing, 2009.

Taylor, Stuart Jr. "Hinckley 'Historical' Shooting to Win Love." *New York Times*, July 9, 1982. https://www.nytimes.com/1982/07/09/us/hinckley-hails-historical-shooting-to-win-love.html.

"This Day in History: April 30, 1993." *History*. Accessed July 18, 2021. https://www.history.com/this-day-in-history/tennis-star-monica-seles-stabbed.

"This Day in History: September 9, Alice B. Toklas Moves in Permanently with Gertrude Stein." *History*. Accessed July 18, 2021. https://www.history.com/this-day-in-history/alice-b-toklas-moves-in-permanently-with-gertrude-stein.

Thomas, Bob. *Liberace: The True Story*. New York: St. Martin's Press, 1988.

"Thomas 'Stonewall' Jackson—Facts, Bio, and Information on the Confederate General." *Historynet*. Last modified 2021. https://www.historynet.com/stonewall-jackson.

"Tom Arnold Biography." *Biography*. Accessed July 20, 2021. https://web.archive.org/web/20091005003320/http://www.biography.com/articles/Tom-Arnold-224913.

Touponce, William R. *Frank Herbert*. Boston: Twayne Publishers, 1988.

"Tupac Shakur: 1971–1996." *Biography*. Last modified January 14, 2020. https://www.biography.com/musician/tupac-shakur.

Tyson, Mike, and Larry Sloman. *Undisputed Truth: Mike Tyson*. New York: Penguin Group, 2013.

"Vladimir Lenin 1870–1924." *BBC History*. Last modified 2014. http://www.bbc.co.uk/history/historic_figures/lenin_vladimir.shtml.

Watson, Steven. *Factory Made: Warhol and the Sixties*. New York: Pantheon Books, 2003.

Watts, Steven. *Mr. Playboy: Hugh Hefner and the American Dream*. Hoboken, NJ: John Wiley and Sons, 2008.

Weir, Alison. *Henry VIII: The King and His Court*. New York: Ballantine Books, 2001.

Weir, Alison. *The Life of Elizabeth I*. New York: Ballantine Books, 1998.

Weller, Sheila. *Raging Heart: The Intimate Story of the Tragic Marriage of O. J. Simpson and Nicole Brown Simpson*. New York: Pocket Books, 1995.

Wels, Susan. *Amelia Earhart: The Thrill of It*. Philadelphia: Running Press, 2009.

Wenner, Jann S., and Corey Seymour. *Gonzo: The Life of Hunter S. Thompson*. New York: Little, Brown & Company, 2007.

White, Barbara Ehrlich. *Renoir: An Intimate Biography*. London: Thames and Hudson, 2017.

Wiener, Jan C. *The Assassination of Heydrich*. New York: Grossman Publishers, 1969.

Wolff, Cynthia Griffin. *Emily Dickinson*. New York: Alfred A. Knopf, 1986.

Woo, Elaine. "Eugene Landy, 71, Psychologist Criticized for Relationship with Troubled Beach Boy Brian Wilson." *LA Times*, March 29, 2006. https://www.latimes.com/archives/la-xpm-2006-mar-29-me-landy29-story.html.

Wood, Ean. *The Josephine Baker Story*. London: Sanctuary Publishing, 2000.

Wydra, Thilo. *Grace: A Biography*. New York: Skyhorse Publishing, 2014.

Yang, Allie, and Gail Deutsch. "Bonny Lee Bakley Had a Remarkable Story That Played a Big Role at Her Husband Robert Blake's Murder Trial." *ABC News*, January 11, 2019. https://abcnews.go.com/US/bonny-lee-bakley-remarkable-story-played-big-role/story?id=60056830.

Zackheim, Michele. *Einstein's Daughter: The Search for Lieserl*. New York: Riverhead, 1999.

To Write to the Author

If you wish to contact the author or would like more information about this book, please write to the author in care of Llewellyn Worldwide Ltd. and we will forward your request. Both the author and the publisher appreciate hearing from you and learning of your enjoyment of this book and how it has helped you. Llewellyn Worldwide Ltd. cannot guarantee that every letter written to the author can be answered, but all will be forwarded. Please write to:

Wendell C. Perry
℅ Llewellyn Worldwide
2143 Wooddale Drive
Woodbury, MN 55125-2989
Please enclose a self-addressed stamped envelope for reply,
or $1.00 to cover costs. If outside the U.S.A., enclose
an international postal reply coupon.

Many of Llewellyn's authors have websites with additional information and resources. For more information, please visit our website at http://www.llewellyn.com.